PICA

ELITE

f an artist.

an artist.

TYPE-CASTER

UNIVERSAL COPYFITTING

Stanley Rice

VNR *Van Nostrand Reinhold Company*
New York   Cincinnati   Toronto   London   Melbourne

For Leslie and Joel

Copyright © 1980 by Litton Educational Publishing, Inc.
Library of Congress Catalog Card Number 79-21969
ISBN 0-442-22565-2

Printed in the United States of America

Published by Van Nostrand Reinhold Company
A division of Litton Educational Publishing, Inc.
135 West 50th Street, New York, NY 10020, U.S.A.

Van Nostrand Reinhold Limited
1410 Birchmount Road
Scarborough, Ontario M1P 2E7, Canada

Van Nostrand Reinhold Australia Pty. Ltd.
17 Queen Street
Mitcham, Victoria 3132, Australia

Van Nostrand Reinhold Company Limited
Molly Millars Lane
Wokingham, Berkshire, England

16 15 14 13 12 11 10 9 8 7 6 5 4 3 2 1

Library of Congress Cataloging in Publication Data

Rice, Stanley.
  Type-caster.

    1. Printing, Practical—Copyfitting.
    2. Type-setting. I. Title.
Z253.R46   686.2'25   79-21969
ISBN 0-442-22565-2

Contents

Introduction

This book contains a flexible, easy, and universally applicable method of copyfitting type—any typeface whatever, to any specifications, now or in the future, from any source, using any typesetting method. This introduction will provide some orientation and background, and directions for using this book. (Skip to the summary instructions on the use of the main table, page 10, if you do not want background.)

A good copyfitting method should start with available and unambiguous information and should provide, with minimum effort, all the information necessary to fit manuscript copy to modern typesetting.

Until now, designers and typographers have not had a method that covers the complete job of fitting, especially for modern typefaces and typesetting. It is often necessary to search out many local sources of information, and even then it may be difficult to get the job done. Many of the newer systems of typesetting have not kept up with their own typographic development in terms of copyfitting information. Typeface names, the traditional method of identification, are nowadays often uninformative, confusing, and misleading. There are typefaces with the same name but with rather different designs, and other faces with basically the same design but different names. Some even have the same name and design but somewhat different fitting characteristics when set on different machines. This is all needlessly perplexing, and leads to unneccessary difficulty and error.

Most copyfitting problems concern type area, but traditional fitting methods have stopped at providing character counts for common lengths of even-pica lines. In fact, the strategies for solving many problems of type fitting have been left to the typographer. This book provides new kinds of help.

The lower case alphabet length
Other than the specifications supplied by the designer, what information is required for copyfitting? Only this—the length in points of the lower

1

case alphabet, from a to z, for the typeface and size proposed (including any proposed modifications of horizontal set size and/or full text letterspacing or kerning). Everything else is derived from that.

The alphabet length is "raw data," and if necessary the designer can measure a printed alphabet, which will properly reflect whatever modern options of fractional sizes, set changes, or letterspacing may be employed in any particular case. (For special jobs, an alphabet can be set to specification.)

The familiar "characters per pica" value is not raw data, and the designer cannot measure it. Its value is derived from the alphabet length by rather complex methods. It depends on letter width values, and on the actual frequencies of characters and spaces in written English. Its value, for somewhat closely spaced, normal sentence-style English text, is approximately 342 divided by the alphabet length, which is the relationship used for the tables in this book.

If you specify the type for a job, you probably know the name of the typeface you use, the source, the machine on which it will be set, the size, and the body. But to use Table 1 in this book, for area copyfitting, all you need to know is: (1) a lower case alphabet length, or characters per pica value, and (2) a proposed type body (size plus leading). You can enter the table with either an alphabet length, the left-most column, or the nearest characters per pica value, in the right-most column.

A characters per pica value is provided for each alphabet length, and there is a table of characters per line, in half-picas, for common text lengths, Table 4. Thus, this book offers what traditional copyfitting methods provide—plus a great deal more.

Area copyfitting—Table 1

How many characters will fit into this *area*, given these specifications? How big an *area* will be required for this copy, given these specifications? These questions involve problems of area copyfitting. Their answers are the strength of Table 1.

Any rectangular area is equivalent to its width times its depth. With this table, type area can be measured in picas, in inches, or in centimeters. Picas are most commonly used, but inches may sometimes be handy for editors or authors, and centimeters may soon be necessary. (For easy multiplication and division, it is most convenient to express fractional parts of dimensions as decimals.)

Picas and half-picas of width and depth are sufficiently accurate for most area measurements, but this table provides for even more accuracy.

Close calculation may sometimes be desirable when a very accurate character count of the manuscript is available.

For the more accurate type area measurements, the width can be specified to any type-settable fraction of a pica, and the depth can be expressed as the exact depth of an even number of type lines, of the type body proposed. These depth values can easily be looked up in Table 5 (p. 54.)

The designer can thus use very accurate area measurements, as may seem required, and the accuracy of the tables will fully reflect the increased accuracy of measurement (see Example A under Examples using Table 1: Area Copyfitting, later in this section).

Typical problems of copyfitting

There are three general types of problems in most copyfitting. They are based on the following three factors:

1. Number of characters to be set.
2. Area to be covered by type.
3. Typesetting specifications, including typeface, type size (or the "set size" if different from the vertical size), body (size plus leading), and any full-text letterspacing or kerning.

Given any two of these factors, the third can be determined.

Problem type A: Given factors 2 and 3, what is factor 1? In book-style typography, the number of characters per page, or other type area, must usually be found.

Problem type B: Given factors 1 and 3, what is factor 2? In advertising and similar commercial typography, the area required for a given piece of copy must often be found.

Problem type C: Given factors 1 and 2, what is factor 3? In any field of typography, the adjustment of typographic specifications, to the characters in the copy and the area allowed, requires the possible adjustment of several interacting design factors. Since this adjustment can involve many choices, a method, such as presented here, is required, to provide quick results for any option.

In this book, the alphabet length (or characters per pica value) and the type body are the only keys necessary to solve the above problems. The alphabet length reflects any type size, including any fractional size and any adjustments of set or letterspacing. Leading choices (type body) are provided in half-point increments. From these two keys, the table provides what is needed.

Table 1:   Area copyfitting

Table 1 concerns area copyfitting. It provides simple methods for dealing with the three general types of problems. It is for condensed 5-point typefaces to expanded 12-point faces, and covers a minimum of zero-to-three points leading-range for the small sizes and a minimum of zero-to-four points for the larger sizes (in half-point leading increments).

The left-most column of Table 1 (column 1) is the alphabet length in points, and the right-most column (column 7) shows the corresponding characters per pica value. Column 2 (text sizes) indicates, for general information only, the approximate range of text type sizes covered by any given alphabet length. Alphabet length 115, for example, may apply to various text typefaces of different designs, from a rather wide 9 point to a condensed 11 point. *The size indication is for general information only and is not actually necessary to, or used at all in, the copyfitting method.*

Column 3 is the type body (type size and associated leading). Columns 1, 3, and 7 are in bold because these values are used to enter the tables. Columns 4, 5, and 6 are the "factors," for 1 square pica, 1 square inch, and 1 square centimeter—for the alphabet length and leading shown on that line. They represent the type characters in one unit, and are to be multiplied by total area units of the same kind to obtain total characters for the area.

Examples using Table 1:   Area copyfitting

Several examples using Table 1 will illustrate the simplicity of this method. Follow the steps, perhaps duplicating them on a pocket calculator.

Example A: Illustrating problem type A—given type specifications and the area, find characters. For now we shall consider area depth to the nearest half-pica only. Assume a page, or other proposed type area, of 26.5 picas wide by 42 picas deep. Thus, the area is 26.5×42 or 1113 square picas. We choose a face with an alphabet length of 114 points (e.g., 9 Garamond book) and a type body of 11.5 points. How many characters will fit into this area?

In Table 1, we go directly to the alphabet length (114) and to the body (11.5) for all necessary information on one line. We note the factor for 1 square pica (because we are dealing with an area in square picas), which is 3.13 (characters per square pica). On the calculator we multiply the area of 1113 square picas by the factor of 3.13. This gives the total characters for the area—3484 characters.

The problem is answered in a few seconds with almost no trouble, and it is accurate enough for most purposes. But, for a type body of 11.5 points, we have used an approximate depth, and we can easily be more accurate if necessary. In Table 5 (depth of type area), we can see that, using an $11\frac{1}{2}$ point body, the depth closest to 42 picas is 41.22 picas.* To obtain the *most accurate* answer, the area should be calculated using the depth of 41.22 picas instead of 42 picas.

The depth of 41.22 times the width gives the most accurate area. That area times the factor for one square pica gives the closest approximation for characters to fit into the area:

$$26.5 \times 41.22 \times 3.13 = 3419.$$

The more correct depth made a difference of less than 2%. It will seldom be greater, although the error is not strictly predictable because it depends on the way the type body and setting area are defined. A large type body and small depth are liable to larger error. In any case, this more precise method, using exact depth, is required mainly when a very accurate count of characters has been made.

Table 1 can also be used with inches and centimeters. An estimate in inches of the area in example A would be about $4\ 3/8 \times 7$, making the area $4.375 \times 7 = 30.6$ square inches. This, times the factor for 1 square inch (113), gives 3458 characters, which is close to the first estimate of 3484 done in square picas. (Such minor differences are caused by difficulties of exact measurement.)

The same area measured in centimeters would be about 11.1×17.7, or 196.47 square centimeters. This, multiplied by the factor for one square centimeter (17.5), gives 3438 characters, which is close to the other estimates. (The exact depth method described above is not applicable, of course, when measuring in inches or centimeters.)

Nonrectangular areas.

This method can be efficiently used to estimate characters to fit nonrectangular areas of many kinds, in picas, inches, or centimeters. For "regular" areas, formulas such as the following can be used to calculate the units of area:

parallelogram: width of top line times depth.

triangle: $\frac{1}{2}$ the width of the base times depth.

---

*This is worked out as follows: 42 picas $\times$ 12 points divided by 11.5 points = 43.83 lines deep. Dropping the fractional line, multiply 43×11.5 and divide by 12 to get the depth of 41.22 picas. Table 5 provides an easier way to do this.

trapezoid: $\frac{1}{2}$ the height times the width of the top line times the width of the bottom line.

regular polygon: $\frac{1}{2}$ the perpendicular from the center to any side times the perimeter.

circle: 3.14 times the radius squared.

In fact, the area of any irregular shape may easily be determined in picas, inches, or centimeters. (Picas will normally be the most accurate.) Simply lay a sheet of transparent, six-lines-to-the-inch graph paper over the irregular area and count the squares.

Example B: Illustrating problem type B—given number of characters and type specifications, find the area required. Assume a given amount of copy (3418 characters) to be set with a typeface having an alphabet length of 114 points and a body of 11.5 points. To use Table 1, it is not necessary to know the name of a typeface or its size, although this would normally be known by the one who picked it. It might be the 9 Garamond Book, or any of several others that fit the same.

Table 1 is entered, first with the alphabet length (114) and then the body (11.5). As before, the factor for 1 square pica is 3.13. But this time we *divide* the factor into the 3418 characters to be set, giving 1092, which is the area required for the setting, in square picas.

This area can have many possible shapes reflecting different widths and depths. It can even be completely irregular. If it is rectangular, we can pick any width and divide it into the area total to get a corresponding depth, or vice versa. If the width is to be 26.5, the depth will have to be 1092 divided by 26.5, or 41.2 picas, which we know to be correct.

If it is more convenient for the area to be expressed in inches or centimeters, the characters can be divided by the appropriate factor from Table 1.

Example C: Illustrating problem type C—given the characters to be set and the area, find the type specifications. Since many sets of specifications may answer the requirements, this problem is one of design judgment and optimization.

Assume the familiar type area of 26.5 × 42 picas, or 1113 square picas. Also assume that 3600 characters are to be fitted into this area, filling the entire space as closely as possible.

First, we make a guess at the specifications, based on preference or job requirements. We may propose 9/12 Janson with an alphabet length of

115 points. We enter Table 1, as usual, with the alphabet length (115) and the body (12), and find a factor of 2.97 for one square pica. This we *divide* into the required characters to get the area $3600 \div 2.97 = 1212$ square picas are area required. This is more than the area allowed, so we must adjust the setting to make it more compact. We can shorten the alphabet length, subtract from the leading, or both. We could change the typeface, size, or text kerning, but the leading is the most obvious and the easiest to change.

To subtract from the leading, look one line down in the table (the 11.5 body). There the factor is 3.10. Dividing this into the characters gives us 1161 square picas of required area ($3600 \div 3.10 = 1161$). But we are still over the specified 1113 square picas.

Decreasing leading again to 11-point body (looking one line down in the table) we get the factor 3.24, and $3600 \div 3.24 = 1111$ square picas. This is, coincidentally, very close to the specified 1113. So we can set the copy $9/11 \times 26.5$ picas, and it should be about 42 picas deep.

Accuracy in copyfitting

Given accurate measurement of the lower case alphabet and of areas, these tables provide very accurate solutions—when the average word space produced by the justification system is about three to the em. This is generally regarded as "normal" spacing. However, the average word space may often vary in actual setting. It depends on the justification methods of the various composition systems, and more especially on the relation of type size to setting width in each individual case. The narrower the column and the larger the type, the more the average word space is likely to increase in size. The smaller the type and the wider the measure, the more "normal" the word space will usually be.

Since the word space is the most frequent "character" in written English (about 37% more frequent than the next most frequent character—the "e"), any variation from the three-to-em average word space will show up in variations of copyfitting. At present the accuracy of character counts is seldom sufficient to make any compensation for word space variation worth while except when setting a considerable amount of copy to short measures, as in newspapers and magazines.

Note: When setting considerable magazine or other material to short measures (less than about 24 ems, e.g., 10 point to less than 20 picas), and especially accurate castoff is required, use Table 1 in the following way:

Enter the table using the right-hand column with a characters per pica figure that is known to be accurate for the size, measure, and typesetting system. If the figure is not known, count all characters and spaces in at least 25 lines set to the measure by the system in question. Divide by the measure and find the average characters per pica figure to use with the table. Then use the table in the normal way.

A rough alternative is to subtract 3% from character counts with lines of about 20–25 ems, and subtract 5% from counts with lines of about 15–20 ems. But this will not take into account the justification and hyphenation effects in the typesetting system.

Note that nonjustified text, if hyphenated normally, fits the same as justified text. If it is not hyphenated, approximately 2–3% may be added to the space required for justified text.

Following Table 1, for area copyfitting, are other useful tables. Table 2 gives characters per pica for display sizes (over 12 point, based on initial cap and lower case). Table 3 gives characters per pica for capital letters. Table 4 gives characters per line by alphabet length for text sizes to half-pica measures, a more detailed version of the traditional copyfitting table. Table 5 gives exact depth in decimal picas for any given number of lines, providing exact area or page depth at a glance.

Since large sizes and capital letters are not normally used in area composition of text, only characters per pica is required to copyfit them. This is multiplied by the measure to give the number of characters that will fit in that measure. Or it can be divided into the characters to give the measure required to set them.

Appendix A: *Castoff-related programs for programmable pocket calculators*

For those interested in figuring out some special applications of castoff in their own work, the programmable calculator is a painless way to do so. It can be very useful for writing special-purpose tables that can make many jobs easier. The programs in this appendix are written in a simple and generalized form easily comprehended by the beginner, and will suggest ways of solving many similar problems. Programmable calculators are becoming less expensive and more available all the time, and more people are now able to work with them.

Appendix B: *A program in Basic to generate tailored tables of castoff results*

Although the tables in this book provide a universal solution to the general problems of copyfitting, more specifically tailored tables answering a particular range of problems for specific trimmed sizes, or other publishing requirements, may also be desirable. Most publishers own or have access to a computer with a line printer. This program will enable them to write a "book" of tables for their special needs, a book that will be composed in less than 10 minutes, depending on length.

Appendix C: Table 6
This is a "tailored table" written by the program in Appendix B, giving some fitting options for the common 6″×9″ trimmed size.

Appendix D: Forms to facilitate castoff*
Characters per line from characters per pica.
Book estimate form and page makeup guide.

Appendix E: Representative alphabet lengths

Appendix F: Points to millimeters, and millimeters to points

*   *   *   *

As the reader will discover, there is almost no problem of copyfitting that this book will not solve easily and accurately, for any typesetting system and for any specifications. Copyfitting is, after all, mainly a necessary nuisance, and it is hoped that this book can make things a good deal easier, as well as more accurate.

S.R.

*From *Book Design*: *Systematic Aspects* by Stanley Rice (Bowker).

HOW TO USE TABLE 1:   AREA COPYFITTING

Alphabet length (or characters per pica) and type body size are all the data needed to use this table.

*TO FIND THE NUMBER OF CHARACTERS THAT CAN BE SET
IN A GIVEN AREA (e.g., characters per page):*
1. Decide whether to measure area in square picas, inches, or centimeters.
2. If measuring in square picas, and great accuracy is not required, simply use depth measured to the nearest half-pica. If the greatest accuracy is required, consult Table 5 to get the exact depth for an even number of type lines.
3. Multiply the area width times depth to get square units of area.
4. Enter Table 1 with alphabet length* (left column), or nearest characters per pica (right column). Find the type body (column 3). On that line read the factor for the kind of units being used for area.
5. Multiply that factor times the square units of area to get the number of characters that can be set in the area.

B

*TO FIND THE AREA REQUIRED TO SET A GIVEN NUMBER OF
CHARACTERS AS SPECIFIED:*
1. From specifications get the alphabet length or characters per pica (for the type size) and the type body.
2. Enter Table 1 with these, and note the factor for the square units to be used for area (picas, inches, centimeters).
3. Divide the characters to be set by this factor, which will give the square units needed to set the copy as specified.
4. Divide the square units by a width to find a depth, or by depth to find a width. (If the area is not acceptable, type specifications must be changed.)

*NOTE: Always use the alphabet length or the characters per pica figure for the *set* size specified, *if* that is different from the vertical type size. For full-text letterspacing, negative or positive, you can adjust the alphabet length by adding or subtracting 26 times the letterspace expressed in points (when alphabet length is known only for normal spacing).

C

TO FIND TYPE SPECIFICATIONS, GIVEN BOTH THE AREA
TO BE FILLED AND THE NUMBER OF CHARACTERS TO BE SET:

1. Start with type specifications for an ideal typesetting.
2. Enter Table 1 with alphabet length (or characters per pica) and the type body specified.
3. Note the factor for the units in which area is specified.
4. Multiply the factor times the square units of area to find the number of characters that will fill that area.
5. Compare the characters that *will* fill the area to the characters that are *required* to fill the area. Note whether more or fewer characters are needed.
6. Adjust the specifications to get more or fewer characters in that area. Then consult Table 1 again. (Usually this simply means looking up or down a line or so in the same column to find factors for alternative leadings or alphabet lengths.)
7. Use specifications that provide a reasonably close fit, allowing a few more characters than specified, to be safe. (If the specifications that provide correct fit are not acceptable, the area or the number of characters specified must be changed.)

TABLE 1
Area Copyfitting

*From alphabet length or characters-per-pica
and the proposed type body, this table provides*:

Characters per square pica
Characters per square inch
Characters per square centimeter
Characters per pica (from alphabet length)
Alphabet length (from characters per pica)

A/L	Sizes	Body	1 sq.pi.	1 sq.in.	1 sq.cm.	Ch./pi.
60	5–6	9	7.6	274	42.5	5.7
60	5–6	8.5	8.05	290	45	5.7
60	5–6	8	8.55	308	47.7	5.7
60	5–6	7.5	9.12	328	50.8	5.7
60	5–6	7	9.77	352	54.6	5.7
60	5–6	6.5	10.52	379	58.7	5.7
60	5–6	6	11.4	410	63.6	5.7
60	5–6	5.5	12.44	448	69.4	5.7
60	5–6	5	13.68	492	76.3	5.7
61	5–6	9	7.48	269	41.7	5.61
61	5–6	8.5	7.92	285	44.2	5.61
61	5–6	8	8.41	303	47	5.61
61	5–6	7.5	8.97	323	50.1	5.61
61	5–6	7	9.61	346	53.6	5.61
61	5–6	6.5	10.35	373	57.8	5.61
61	5–6	6	11.21	404	62.6	5.61
61	5–6	5.5	12.23	440	68.2	5.61
61	5–6	5	13.46	484	75	5.61
62	5–6	9	7.35	265	41.1	5.52
62	5–6	8.5	7.79	280	43.4	5.52
62	5–6	8	8.27	298	46.2	5.52
62	5–6	7.5	8.83	318	49.3	5.52
62	5–6	7	9.46	340	52.7	5.52
62	5–6	6.5	10.18	367	56.9	5.52
62	5–6	6	11.03	397	61.5	5.52
62	5–6	5.5	12.04	433	67.1	5.52
62	5–6	5	13.24	477	73.9	5.52
63	5–6	9	7.24	261	40.5	5.43
63	5–6	8.5	7.66	276	42.8	5.43
63	5–6	8	8.14	293	45.4	5.43
63	5–6	7.5	8.69	313	48.5	5.43
63	5–6	7	9.31	335	51.9	5.43
63	5–6	6.5	10.02	361	56	5.43
63	5–6	6	10.86	391	60.6	5.43
63	5–6	5.5	11.84	426	66	5.43
63	5–6	5	13.03	469	72.7	5.43
64	5–6	9	7.13	257	39.8	5.34
64	5–6	8.5	7.54	272	42.2	5.34
64	5–6	8	8.02	289	44.8	5.34
64	5–6	7.5	8.55	308	47.7	5.34
64	5–6	7	9.16	330	51.2	5.34
64	5–6	6.5	9.87	355	55	5.34

A/L	Sizes	Body	1 sq.pi.	1 sq.in.	1 sq.cm.	Ch./pi.
64	5–6	6	10.69	385	59.7	**5.34**
64	5–6	5.5	11.66	420	65.1	**5.34**
64	5–6	5	12.83	462	71.6	**5.34**
65	5–6	9	7.02	253	39.2	**5.26**
65	5–6	8.5	7.43	267	41.4	**5.26**
65	5–6	8	7.89	284	44	**5.26**
65	5–6	7.5	8.42	303	47	**5.26**
65	5–6	7	9.02	325	50.4	**5.26**
65	5–6	6.5	9.71	350	54.3	**5.26**
65	5–6	6	10.52	379	58.7	**5.26**
65	5–6	5.5	11.48	413	64	**5.26**
65	5–6	5	12.63	455	70.5	**5.26**
66	5–6	9	6.91	249	38.6	**5.18**
66	5–6	8.5	7.32	263	40.8	**5.18**
66	5–6	8	7.77	200	43.4	**5.18**
66	5–6	7.5	8.29	298	46.2	**5.18**
66	5–6	7	8.88	320	49.6	**5.18**
66	5–6	6.5	9.57	344	53.3	**5.18**
66	5–6	6	10.36	373	57.8	**5.18**
66	5–6	5.5	11.31	407	63.1	**5.18**
66	5–6	5	12.44	448	69.4	**5.18**
67	5–6	9	6.81	245	38	**5.1**
67	5–6	8.5	7.21	259	40.1	**5.1**
67	5–6	8	7.66	276	42.8	**5.1**
67	5–6	7.5	8.17	294	45.6	**5.1**
67	5–6	7	8.75	315	48.8	**5.1**
67	5–6	6.5	9.42	339	52.5	**5.1**
67	5–6	6	10.21	368	57	**5.1**
67	5–6	5.5	11.14	401	62.2	**5.1**
67	5–6	5	12.25	441	68.4	**5.1**
68	5–6	9	6.71	241	37.4	**5.03**
68	5–6	8.5	7.1	256	39.7	**5.03**
68	5–6	8	7.54	272	42.2	**5.03**
68	5–6	7.5	8.05	290	45	**5.03**
68	5–6	7	8.62	310	48.1	**5.03**
68	5–6	6.5	9.29	334	51.8	**5.03**
68	5–6	6	10.06	362	56.1	**5.03**
68	5–6	5.5	10.97	395	61.2	**5.03**
68	5–6	5	12.07	435	67.4	**5.03**
69	5–6	9	6.61	238	36.9	**4.96**
69	5–6	8.5	7	252	39.1	**4.96**

A/L	Sizes	Body	1 sq.pi.	1 sq.in.	1 sq.cm.	Ch./pi.
69	5–6	8	7.43	268	41.5	4.96
69	5–6	7.5	7.93	285	44.2	4.96
69	5–6	7	8.5	306	47.4	4.96
69	5–6	6.5	9.15	329	51	4.96
69	5–6	6	9.91	357	55.3	4.96
69	5–6	5.5	10.81	389	60.3	4.96
69	5–6	5	11.9	428	66.3	4.96
70	5–6	9	6.51	235	36.4	4.89
70	5–6	8.5	6.9	248	38.4	4.89
70	5–6	8	7.33	264	40.9	4.89
70	5–6	7.5	7.82	281	43.6	4.89
70	5–6	7	8.38	302	46.8	4.89
70	5–6	6.5	9.02	325	50.4	4.89
70	5–6	6	9.77	352	54.6	4.89
70	5–6	5.5	10.66	384	59.5	4.89
70	5–6	5	11.73	422	65.4	4.89
71	5–6	9	6.42	231	35.8	4.82
71	5–6	8.5	6.8	245	38	4.82
71	5–6	8	7.23	260	40.3	4.82
71	5–6	7.5	7.71	277	42.9	4.82
71	5–6	7	8.26	297	46	4.82
71	5–6	6.5	8.89	320	49.6	4.82
71	5–6	6	9.63	347	53.8	4.82
71	5–6	5.5	10.51	378	58.6	4.82
71	5–6	5	11.56	416	64.5	4.82
72	5–6	9	6.33	228	35.3	4.75
72	5–6	8.5	6.71	241	37.4	4.75
72	5–6	8	7.13	257	39.8	4.75
72	5–6	7.5	7.6	274	42.5	4.75
72	5–6	7	8.14	293	45.4	4.75
72	5–6	6.5	8.77	316	49	4.75
72	5–6	6	9.5	342	53	4.75
72	5–6	5.5	10.36	373	57.8	4.75
72	5–6	5	11.4	410	63.6	4.75
73	6–7	10	5.62	202	31.3	4.68
73	6–7	9.5	5.92	213	33	4.68
73	6–7	9	6.25	225	34.9	4.68
73	6–7	8.5	6.61	238	36.9	4.68
73	6–7	8	7.03	253	39.2	4.68
73	6–7	7.5	7.5	270	41.9	4.68
73	6–7	7	8.03	289	44.8	4.68
73	6–7	6.5	8.65	311	48.2	4.68

A/L	Sizes	Body	1 sq.pi.	1 sq.in.	1 sq.cm.	Ch./pi.
73	6–7	6	9.37	337	52.2	4.68
74	6–7	10	5.5	200	31	4.62
74	6–7	9.5	5.84	210	32.6	4.62
74	6–7	9	6.16	222	34.4	4.62
74	6–7	8.5	6.52	235	36.4	4.62
74	6–7	8	6.93	250	38.8	4.62
74	6–7	7.5	7.39	266	41.2	4.62
74	6–7	7	7.92	285	44.2	4.62
74	6–7	6.5	8.53	307	47.6	4.62
74	6–7	6	9.24	333	51.6	4.62
75	6–7	10	5.47	197	30.5	4.56
75	6–7	9.5	5.76	207	32.1	4.56
75	6–7	9	6.08	219	33.9	4.56
75	6–7	8.5	6.44	232	36	4.56
75	6–7	8	6.84	246	38.1	4.56
75	6–7	7.5	7.3	263	40.8	4.56
75	6–7	7	7.82	281	43.6	4.56
75	6–7	6.5	8.42	303	47	4.56
75	6–7	6	9.12	328	50.8	4.56
76	6–7	10	5.4	194	30.1	4.5
76	6–7	9.5	5.68	205	31.8	4.5
76	6–7	9	6	216	33.5	4.5
76	6–7	8.5	6.35	229	35.5	4.5
76	6–7	8	6.75	243	37.7	4.5
76	6–7	7.5	7.2	259	40.1	4.5
76	6–7	7	7.71	278	43.1	4.5
76	6–7	6.5	8.31	299	46.3	4.5
76	6–7	6	9	324	50.2	4.5
77	6–7	10	5.33	192	29.8	4.44
77	6–7	9.5	5.61	202	31.3	4.44
77	6–7	9	5.92	213	33	4.44
77	6–7	8.5	6.27	226	35	4.44
77	6–7	8	6.66	240	37.2	4.44
77	6–7	7.5	7.11	256	39.7	4.44
77	6–7	7	7.61	274	42.5	4.44
77	6–7	6.5	8.2	295	45.7	4.44
77	6–7	6	8.88	320	49.6	4.44
78	6–7	10	5.26	189	29.3	4.38
78	6–7	9.5	5.54	199	30.8	4.38
78	6–7	9	5.85	210	32.6	4.38
78	6–7	8.5	6.19	223	34.6	4.38

A/L	Sizes	Body	1 sq.pi.	1 sq.in.	1 sq.cm.	Ch./pi.
78	6–7	8	6.58	237	36.7	4.38
78	6–7	7.5	7.02	253	39.2	4.38
78	6–7	7	7.52	271	42	4.38
78	6–7	6.5	8.09	291	45.1	4.38
78	6–7	6	8.77	316	49	4.38
79	6–7	10	5.19	187	29	4.33
79	6–7	9.5	5.47	197	30.5	4.33
79	6–7	9	5.77	208	32.2	4.33
79	6–7	8.5	6.11	220	34.1	4.33
79	6–7	8	6.49	234	36.3	4.33
79	6–7	7.5	6.93	249	38.6	4.33
79	6–7	7	7.42	267	41.4	4.33
79	6–7	6.5	7.99	288	44.6	4.33
79	6–7	6	8.66	312	48.4	4.33
80	6–7	10	5.13	185	28.7	4.28
80	6–7	9.5	5.4	194	30.1	4.28
80	6–7	9	5.7	205	31.8	4.28
80	6–7	8.5	6.04	217	33.6	4.28
80	6–7	8	6.41	231	35.8	4.28
80	6–7	7.5	6.84	246	38.1	4.28
80	6–7	7	7.33	264	40.9	4.28
80	6–7	6.5	7.89	284	44	4.28
80	6–7	6	8.55	308	47.7	4.28
81	6–8	11	4.61	166	25.7	4.22
81	6–8	10.5	4.83	174	27	4.22
81	6–8	10	5.07	182	28.2	4.22
81	6–8	9.5	5.33	192	29.8	4.22
81	6–8	9	5.63	203	31.5	4.22
81	6–8	8.5	5.96	215	33.3	4.22
81	6–8	8	6.33	228	35.3	4.22
81	6–8	7.5	6.76	243	37.7	4.22
81	6–8	7	7.24	261	40.5	4.22
81	6–8	6.5	7.79	281	43.6	4.22
81	6–8	6	8.44	304	47.1	4.22
82	6–8	11	4.55	164	25.4	4.17
82	6–8	10.5	4.77	172	26.7	4.17
82	6–8	10	5	180	27.9	4.17
82	6–8	9.5	5.27	190	29.5	4.17
82	6–8	9	5.56	200	31	4.17
82	6–8	8.5	5.89	212	32.9	4.17
82	6–8	8	6.26	225	34.9	4.17
82	6–8	7.5	6.67	240	37.2	4.17

A/L	Sizes	Body	1 sq.pi.	1 sq.in.	1 sq.cm.	Ch./pi.
82	6–8	7	7.15	257	39.8	4.17
82	6–8	6.5	7.7	277	42.9	4.17
82	6–8	6	8.34	300	46.5	4.17
83	6–8	11	4.5	162	25.1	4.12
83	6–8	10.5	4.71	170	26.4	4.12
83	6–8	10	4.94	178	27.6	4.12
83	6–8	9.5	5.2	187	29	4.12
83	6–8	9	5.49	198	30.7	4.12
83	6–8	8.5	5.82	209	32.4	4.12
83	6–8	8	6.18	223	34.6	4.12
83	6–8	7.5	6.59	237	36.7	4.12
83	6–8	7	7.06	254	39.4	4.12
83	6–8	6.5	7.61	274	42.5	4.12
83	6–8	6	8.24	297	46	4.12
84	6–8	11	4.44	160	24.8	4.07
84	6–8	10.5	4.65	168	26	4.07
84	6–8	10	4.89	176	27.3	4.07
84	6–8	9.5	5.14	185	28.7	4.07
84	6–8	9	5.43	195	30.2	4.07
84	6–8	8.5	5.75	207	32.1	4.07
84	6–8	8	6.11	220	34.1	4.07
84	6–8	7.5	6.51	235	36.4	4.07
84	6–8	7	6.98	251	38.9	4.07
84	6–8	6.5	7.52	271	42	4.07
84	6–8	6	8.14	293	45.4	4.07
85	7–8	11	4.39	158	24.5	4.02
85	7–8	10.5	4.6	166	25.7	4.02
85	7–8	10	4.83	174	27	4.02
85	7–8	9.5	5.08	183	28.4	4.02
85	7–8	9	5.36	193	29.9	4.02
85	7–8	8.5	5.68	204	31.6	4.02
85	7–8	8	6.04	217	33.6	4.02
85	7–8	7.5	6.44	232	36	4.02
85	7–8	7	6.9	248	38.4	4.02
86	7–8	11	4.34	156	24.2	3.98
86	7–8	10.5	4.54	164	25.4	3.98
86	7–8	10	4.77	172	26.7	3.98
86	7–8	9.5	5.02	181	28.1	3.98
86	7–8	9	5.3	191	29.6	3.98
86	7–8	8.5	5.61	202	31.3	3.98
86	7–8	8	5.97	215	33.3	3.98
86	7–8	7.5	6.36	229	35.5	3.98

A/L	Sizes	Body	1 sq.pi.	1 sq.in.	1 sq.cm.	Ch./pi.
86	7–8	7	6.82	245	38	3.98
87	7–8	11	4.29	154	23.9	3.93
87	7–8	10.5	4.49	162	25.1	3.93
87	7–8	10	4.72	170	26.4	3.93
87	7–8	9.5	4.97	179	27.7	3.93
87	7–8	9	5.24	189	29.3	3.93
87	7–8	8.5	5.55	200	31	3.93
87	7–8	8	5.9	212	32.9	3.93
87	7–8	7.5	6.29	226	35	3.93
87	7–8	7	6.74	243	37.7	3.93
88	7–8	11	4.24	153	23.7	3.89
88	7–8	10.5	4.44	160	24.8	3.89
88	7–8	10	4.66	168	26	3.89
88	7–8	9.5	4.91	177	27.4	3.89
88	7–8	9	5.18	187	29	3.89
88	7–8	8.5	5.49	198	30.7	3.89
88	7–8	8	5.83	210	32.6	3.89
88	7–8	7.5	6.22	224	34.7	3.89
88	7–8	7	6.66	240	37.2	3.89
89	7–8	11	4.19	151	23.4	3.84
89	7–8	10.5	4.39	158	24.5	3.84
89	7–8	10	4.61	166	25.7	3.84
89	7–8	9.5	4.85	175	27.1	3.84
89	7–8	9	5.12	184	28.5	3.84
89	7–8	8.5	5.42	195	30.2	3.84
89	7–8	8	5.76	208	32.2	3.84
89	7–8	7.5	6.15	221	34.3	3.84
89	7–8	7	6.59	237	36.7	3.84
90	7–9	12	3.8	137	21.2	3.8
90	7–9	11.5	3.97	143	22.2	3.8
90	7–9	11	4.15	149	23.1	3.8
90	7–9	10.5	4.34	156	24.2	3.8
90	7–9	10	4.56	164	25.4	3.8
90	7–9	9.5	4.8	173	26.8	3.8
90	7–9	9	5.07	182	28.2	3.8
90	7–9	8.5	5.36	193	29.9	3.8
90	7–9	8	5.7	205	31.8	3.8
90	7–9	7.5	6.08	219	33.9	3.8
90	7–9	7	6.51	235	36.4	3.8
91	7–9	12	3.76	135	20.9	3.76
91	7–9	11.5	3.92	141	21.9	3.76

A/L	Sizes	Body	1 sq.pi.	1 sq.in.	1 sq.cm.	Ch./pi.
91	7–9	11	4.1	148	22.9	3.76
91	7–9	10.5	4.3	155	24	3.76
91	7–9	10	4.51	162	25.1	3.76
91	7–9	9.5	4.75	171	26.5	3.76
91	7–9	9	5.01	180	27.9	3.76
91	7–9	8.5	5.31	191	29.6	3.76
91	7–9	8	5.64	203	31.5	3.76
91	7–9	7.5	6.01	216	33.5	3.76
91	7–9	7	6.44	232	36	3.76
92	7–9	12	3.72	134	20.8	3.72
92	7–9	11.5	3.88	140	21.7	3.72
92	7–9	11	4.06	146	22.6	3.72
92	7–9	10.5	4.25	153	23.7	3.72
92	7–9	10	4.46	161	25	3.72
92	7–9	9.5	4.7	169	26.2	3.72
92	7–9	9	4.96	178	27.6	3.72
92	7–9	8.5	5.25	189	29.3	3.72
92	7–9	8	5.58	201	31.2	3.72
92	7–9	7.5	5.95	214	33.2	3.72
92	7–9	7	6.37	229	35.5	3.72
93	7–9	12	3.68	132	20.5	3.68
93	7–9	11.5	3.84	138	21.4	3.68
93	7–9	11	4.01	144	22.3	3.68
93	7–9	10.5	4.2	151	23.4	3.68
93	7–9	10	4.41	159	24.6	3.68
93	7–9	9.5	4.65	167	25.9	3.68
93	7–9	9	4.9	177	27.4	3.68
93	7–9	8.5	5.19	187	29	3.68
93	7–9	8	5.52	199	30.8	3.68
93	7–9	7.5	5.88	212	32.9	3.68
93	7–9	7	6.3	227	35.2	3.68
94	7–9	12	3.64	131	20.3	3.64
94	7–9	11.5	3.8	137	21.2	3.64
94	7–9	11	3.97	143	22.2	3.64
94	7–9	10.5	4.16	150	23.3	3.64
94	7–9	10	4.37	157	24.3	3.64
94	7–9	9.5	4.6	165	25.6	3.64
94	7–9	9	4.85	175	27.1	3.64
94	7–9	8.5	5.14	185	28.7	3.64
94	7–9	8	5.46	196	30.4	3.64
94	7–9	7.5	5.82	210	32.6	3.64
94	7–9	7	6.24	225	34.9	3.64

A/L	Sizes	Body	1 sq.pi.	1 sq.in.	1 sq.cm.	Ch./pi.
95	7–9	12	3.6	130	20.2	3.6
95	7–9	11.5	3.76	135	20.9	3.6
95	7–9	11	3.93	141	21.9	3.6
95	7–9	10.5	4.11	148	22.9	3.6
95	7–9	10	4.32	156	24.2	3.6
95	7–9	9.5	4.55	164	25.4	3.6
95	7–9	9	4.8	173	26.8	3.6
95	7–9	8.5	5.08	183	28.4	3.6
95	7–9	8	5.4	194	30.1	3.6
95	7–9	7.5	5.76	207	32.1	3.6
95	7–9	7	6.17	222	34.4	3.6
96	7–9	12	3.56	128	19.8	3.56
96	7–9	11.5	3.72	134	20.8	3.56
96	7–9	11	3.89	140	21.7	3.56
96	7–9	10.5	4.07	147	22.8	3.56
96	7–9	10	4.28	154	23.9	3.56
96	7–9	9.5	4.5	162	25.1	3.56
96	7–9	9	4.75	171	26.5	3.56
96	7–9	8.5	5.03	181	28.1	3.56
96	7–9	8	5.34	192	29.8	3.56
96	7–9	7.5	5.7	205	31.8	3.56
96	7–9	7	6.11	220	34.1	3.56
97	7–9	12	3.53	127	19.7	3.53
97	7–9	11.5	3.68	132	20.5	3.53
97	7–9	11	3.85	138	21.4	3.53
97	7–9	10.5	4.03	145	22.5	3.53
97	7–9	10	4.23	152	23.6	3.53
97	7–9	9.5	4.45	160	24.8	3.53
97	7–9	9	4.7	169	26.2	3.53
97	7–9	8.5	4.98	179	27.7	3.53
97	7–9	8	5.29	190	29.5	3.53
97	7–9	7.5	5.64	203	31.5	3.53
97	7–9	7	6.04	218	33.8	3.53
98	7–9	12	3.49	126	19.5	3.49
98	7–9	11.5	3.64	131	20.3	3.49
98	7–9	11	3.81	137	21.2	3.49
98	7–9	10.5	3.99	144	22.3	3.49
98	7–9	10	4.19	151	23.4	3.49
98	7–9	9.5	4.41	159	24.6	3.49
98	7–9	9	4.65	168	26	3.49
98	7–9	8.5	4.93	177	27.4	3.49
98	7–9	8	5.23	188	29.1	3.49
98	7–9	7.5	5.58	201	31.2	3.49

A/L	Sizes	Body	1 sq.pi.	1 sq.in.	1 sq.cm.	Ch./pi.
98	7–9	7	5.98	215	33.3	3.49
99	7–9	12	3.45	124	19.2	3.45
99	7–9	11.5	3.6	130	20.2	3.45
99	7–9	11	3.77	136	21.1	3.45
99	7–9	10.5	3.95	142	22	3.45
99	7–9	10	4.15	149	23.1	3.45
99	7–9	9.5	4.36	157	24.3	3.45
99	7–9	9	4.61	166	25.7	3.45
99	7–9	8.5	4.88	176	27.3	3.45
99	7–9	8	5.18	187	29	3.45
99	7–9	7.5	5.53	199	30.8	3.45
99	7–9	7	5.92	213	33	3.45
100	8–10	14	2.93	106	16.4	3.42
100	8–10	13.5	3.04	109	16.9	3.42
100	8–10	13	3.16	114	17.7	3.42
100	8–10	12.5	3.28	118	18.3	3.42
100	8–10	12	3.42	123	19.1	3.42
100	8–10	11.5	3.57	128	19.8	3.42
100	8–10	11	3.73	134	20.8	3.42
100	8–10	10.5	3.91	141	21.9	3.42
100	8–10	10	4.1	148	22.9	3.42
100	8–10	9.5	4.32	156	24.2	3.42
100	8–10	9	4.56	164	25.4	3.42
100	8–10	8.5	4.83	174	27	3.42
100	8–10	8	5.13	185	28.7	3.42
101	8–10	14	2.9	104	16.1	3.39
101	8–10	13.5	3.01	108	16.7	3.39
101	8–10	13	3.13	113	17.5	3.39
101	8–10	12.5	3.25	117	18.1	3.39
101	8–10	12	3.39	122	18.9	3.39
101	8–10	11.5	3.53	127	19.7	3.39
101	8–10	11	3.69	133	20.6	3.39
101	8–10	10.5	3.87	139	21.5	3.39
101	8–10	10	4.06	146	22.6	3.39
101	8–10	9.5	4.28	154	23.9	3.39
101	8–10	9	4.51	163	25.3	3.39
101	8–10	8.5	4.78	172	26.7	3.39
101	8–10	8	5.08	183	28.4	3.39
102	8–10	14	2.87	103	16	3.35
102	8–10	13.5	2.98	107	16.6	3.35
102	8–10	13	3.1	111	17.2	3.35
102	8–10	12.5	3.22	116	18	3.35

A/L	Sizes	Body	1 sq.pi.	1 sq.in.	1 sq.cm.	Ch./pi.
102	8–10	12	3.35	121	18.8	3.35
102	8–10	11.5	3.5	126	19.5	3.35
102	8–10	11	3.66	132	20.5	3.35
102	8–10	10.5	3.83	138	21.4	3.35
102	8–10	10	4.02	145	22.5	3.35
102	8–10	9.5	4.24	152	23.6	3.35
102	8–10	9	4.47	161	25	3.35
102	8–10	8.5	4.73	170	26.4	3.35
102	8–10	8	5.03	181	28.1	3.35
103	8–10	14	2.85	102	15.8	3.32
103	8–10	13.5	2.95	106	16.4	3.32
103	8–10	13	3.06	110	17.1	3.32
103	8–10	12.5	3.19	115	17.8	3.32
103	8–10	12	3.32	120	18.6	3.32
103	8–10	11.5	3.46	125	19.4	3.32
103	8–10	11	3.62	130	20.2	3.32
103	8–10	10.5	3.79	137	21.2	3.32
103	8–10	10	3.98	143	22.2	3.32
103	8–10	9.5	4.19	151	23.4	3.32
103	8–10	9	4.43	159	24.6	3.32
103	8–10	8.5	4.69	169	26.2	3.32
103	8–10	8	4.98	179	27.7	3.32
104	8–10	14	2.82	101	15.7	3.29
104	8–10	13.5	2.92	105	16.3	3.29
104	8–10	13	3.04	109	16.9	3.29
104	8–10	12.5	3.16	114	17.7	3.29
104	8–10	12	3.29	118	18.3	3.29
104	8–10	11.5	3.43	124	19.2	3.29
104	8–10	11	3.59	129	20	3.29
104	8–10	10.5	3.76	135	20.9	3.29
104	8–10	10	3.95	142	22	3.29
104	8–10	9.5	4.15	150	23.3	3.29
104	8–10	9	4.38	158	24.5	3.29
104	8–10	8.5	4.64	167	25.9	3.29
104	8–10	8	4.93	178	27.6	3.29
105	8–10	14	2.79	101	15.7	3.26
105	8–10	13.5	2.9	104	16.1	3.26
105	8–10	13	3.01	108	16.7	3.26
105	8–10	12.5	3.13	113	17.5	3.26
105	8–10	12	3.26	117	18.1	3.26
105	8–10	11.5	3.4	122	18.9	3.26
105	8–10	11	3.55	128	19.8	3.26
105	8–10	10.5	3.72	134	20.8	3.26

A/L	Sizes	Body	1 sq.pi.	1 sq.in.	1 sq.cm.	Ch./pi.
105	8–10	10	3.91	141	21.9	3.26
105	8–10	9.5	4.11	148	22.9	3.26
105	8–10	9	4.34	156	24.2	3.26
105	8–10	8.5	4.6	166	25.7	3.26
105	8–10	8	4.89	176	27.3	3.26
106	8–10	14	2.77	100	15.5	3.23
106	8–10	13.5	2.87	103	16	3.23
106	8–10	13	2.98	107	16.6	3.23
106	8–10	12.5	3.1	112	17.4	3.23
106	8–10	12	3.23	116	18	3.23
106	8–10	11.5	3.37	121	18.8	3.23
106	8–10	11	3.52	127	19.7	3.23
106	8–10	10.5	3.69	133	20.6	3.23
106	8–10	10	3.87	139	21.5	3.23
106	8–10	9.5	4.08	147	22.8	3.23
106	8–10	9	4.3	155	24	3.23
106	8–10	8.5	4.55	164	25.4	3.23
106	8–10	8	4.84	174	27	3.23
107	8–10	14	2.74	99	15.3	3.2
107	8–10	13.5	2.84	102	15.8	3.2
107	8–10	13	2.95	106	16.4	3.2
107	8–10	12.5	3.07	110	17.1	3.2
107	8–10	12	3.2	115	17.8	3.2
107	8–10	11.5	3.34	120	18.6	3.2
107	8–10	11	3.49	126	19.5	3.2
107	8–10	10.5	3.65	132	20.5	3.2
107	8–10	10	3.84	138	21.4	3.2
107	8–10	9.5	4.04	145	22.5	3.2
107	8–10	9	4.26	153	23.7	3.2
107	8–10	8.5	4.51	162	25.1	3.2
107	8–10	8	4.79	173	26.8	3.2
108	8–10	14	2.71	98	15.2	3.17
108	8–10	13.5	2.81	101	15.7	3.17
108	8–10	13	2.92	105	16.3	3.17
108	8–10	12.5	3.04	109	16.9	3.17
108	8–10	12	3.17	114	17.7	3.17
108	8–10	11.5	3.3	119	18.4	3.17
108	8–10	11	3.45	124	19.2	3.17
108	8–10	10.5	3.62	130	20.2	3.17
108	8–10	10	3.8	137	21.2	3.17
108	8–10	9.5	4	144	22.3	3.17
108	8–10	9	4.22	152	23.6	3.17
108	8–10	8.5	4.47	161	25	3.17

A/L	Sizes	Body	1 sq.pi.	1 sq.in.	1 sq.cm.	Ch./pi.
108	8–10	**8**	4.75	171	26.5	**3.17**
109	8–10	**14**	2.69	97	15	**3.14**
109	8–10	**13.5**	2.79	100	15.5	**3.14**
109	8–10	**13**	2.9	104	16.1	**3.14**
109	8–10	**12.5**	3.01	108	16.7	**3.14**
109	8–10	**12**	3.14	113	17.5	**3.14**
109	8–10	**11.5**	3.27	118	18.3	**3.14**
109	8–10	**11**	3.42	123	19.1	**3.14**
109	8–10	**10.5**	3.59	129	20	**3.14**
109	8–10	**10**	3.77	136	21.1	**3.14**
109	8–10	**9.5**	3.96	143	22.2	**3.14**
109	8–10	**9**	4.18	151	23.4	**3.14**
109	8–10	**8.5**	4.43	159	24.6	**3.14**
109	8–10	**8**	4.71	169	26.2	**3.14**
110	8–11	**15**	2.49	90	14	**3.11**
110	8–11	**14.5**	2.57	93	14.4	**3.11**
110	8–11	**14**	2.66	96	14.9	**3.11**
110	8–11	**13.5**	2.76	99	15.3	**3.11**
110	8–11	**13**	2.87	103	16	**3.11**
110	8–11	**12.5**	2.98	107	16.6	**3.11**
110	8–11	**12**	3.11	112	17.4	**3.11**
110	8–11	**11.5**	3.24	117	18.1	**3.11**
110	8–11	**11**	3.39	122	18.9	**3.11**
110	8–11	**10.5**	3.55	128	19.8	**3.11**
110	8–11	**10**	3.73	134	20.8	**3.11**
110	8–11	**9.5**	3.93	141	21.9	**3.11**
110	8–11	**9**	4.15	149	23.1	**3.11**
110	8–11	**8.5**	4.39	158	24.5	**3.11**
110	8–11	**8**	4.66	168	26	**3.11**
111	8–11	**15**	2.46	89	13.8	**3.08**
111	8–11	**14.5**	2.55	92	14.3	**3.08**
111	8–11	**14**	2.64	95	14.7	**3.08**
111	8–11	**13.5**	2.74	99	15.3	**3.08**
111	8–11	**13**	2.84	102	15.8	**3.08**
111	8–11	**12.5**	2.96	106	16.4	**3.08**
111	8–11	**12**	3.08	111	17.2	**3.08**
111	8–11	**11.5**	3.22	116	18	**3.08**
111	8–11	**11**	3.36	121	18.8	**3.08**
111	8–11	**10.5**	3.52	127	19.7	**3.08**
111	8–11	**10**	3.7	133	20.6	**3.08**
111	8–11	**9.5**	3.89	140	21.7	**3.08**
111	8–11	**9**	4.11	148	22.9	**3.08**
111	8–11	**8.5**	4.35	157	24.3	**3.08**

A/L	Sizes	Body	1 sq.pi.	1 sq.in.	1 sq.cm.	Ch./pi.
111	8–11	**8**	4.62	166	25.7	**3.08**
112	8–11	**15**	2.44	88	13.6	**3.05**
112	8–11	**14.5**	2.53	91	14.1	**3.05**
112	8–11	**14**	2.62	94	14.6	**3.05**
112	8–11	**13.5**	2.71	98	15.2	**3.05**
112	8–11	**13**	2.82	101	15.7	**3.05**
112	8–11	**12.5**	2.93	106	16.4	**3.05**
112	8–11	**12**	3.05	110	17.1	**3.05**
112	8–11	**11.5**	3.19	115	17.8	**3.05**
112	8–11	**11**	3.33	120	18.6	**3.05**
112	8–11	**10.5**	3.49	126	19.5	**3.05**
112	8–11	**10**	3.66	132	20.5	**3.05**
112	8–11	**9.5**	3.86	139	21.5	**3.05**
112	8–11	**9**	4.07	147	22.8	**3.05**
112	8–11	**8.5**	4.31	155	24	**3.05**
112	8–11	**8**	4.58	165	25.6	**3.05**
113	8–11	**15**	2.42	87	13.5	**3.03**
113	8–11	**14.5**	2.5	90	14	**3.03**
113	8–11	**14**	2.59	93	14.4	**3.03**
113	8–11	**13.5**	2.69	97	15	**3.03**
113	8–11	**13**	2.79	101	15.7	**3.03**
113	8–11	**12.5**	2.91	105	16.3	**3.03**
113	8–11	**12**	3.03	109	16.9	**3.03**
113	8–11	**11.5**	3.16	114	17.7	**3.03**
113	8–11	**11**	3.3	119	18.4	**3.03**
113	8–11	**10.5**	3.46	125	19.4	**3.03**
113	8–11	**10**	3.63	131	20.3	**3.03**
113	8–11	**9.5**	3.82	138	21.4	**3.03**
113	8–11	**9**	4.04	145	22.5	**3.03**
113	8–11	**8.5**	4.27	154	23.9	**3.03**
113	8–11	**8**	4.54	163	25.3	**3.03**
114	9–11	**15**	2.4	86	13.3	**3**
114	9–11	**14.5**	2.48	89	13.8	**3**
114	9–11	**14**	2.57	93	14.4	**3**
114	9–11	**13.5**	2.67	96	14.9	**3**
114	9–11	**13**	2.77	100	15.5	**3**
114	9–11	**12.5**	2.88	104	16.1	**3**
114	9–11	**12**	3	108	16.7	**3**
114	9–11	**11.5**	3.13	113	17.5	**3**
114	9–11	**11**	3.27	118	18.3	**3**
114	9–11	**10.5**	3.43	123	19.1	**3**
114	9–11	**10**	3.6	130	20.2	**3**
114	9–11	**9.5**	3.79	136	21.1	**3**

A/L	Sizes	Body	1 sq.pi.	1 sq.in.	1 sq.cm.	Ch./pi.
114	9–11	**9**	4	144	22.3	**3**
115	9–11	**15**	2.38	86	13.3	**2.97**
115	9–11	**14.5**	2.46	89	13.8	**2.97**
115	9–11	**14**	2.55	92	14.3	**2.97**
115	9–11	**13.5**	2.64	95	14.7	**2.97**
115	9–11	**13**	2.75	99	15.3	**2.97**
115	9–11	**12.5**	2.85	103	16	**2.97**
115	9–11	**12**	2.97	107	16.6	**2.97**
115	9–11	**11.5**	3.1	112	17.4	**2.97**
115	9–11	**11**	3.24	117	18.1	**2.97**
115	9–11	**10.5**	3.4	122	18.9	**2.97**
115	9–11	**10**	3.57	128	19.8	**2.97**
115	9–11	**9.5**	3.76	135	20.9	**2.97**
115	9–11	**9**	3.97	143	22.2	**2.97**
116	9–11	**15**	2.36	85	13.2	**2.95**
116	9–11	**14.5**	2.44	88	13.6	**2.95**
116	9–11	**14**	2.53	91	14.1	**2.95**
116	9–11	**13.5**	2.62	94	14.6	**2.95**
116	9–11	**13**	2.72	98	15.2	**2.95**
116	9–11	**12.5**	2.83	102	15.8	**2.95**
116	9–11	**12**	2.95	106	16.4	**2.95**
116	9–11	**11.5**	3.08	111	17.2	**2.95**
116	9–11	**11**	3.22	116	18	**2.95**
116	9–11	**10.5**	3.37	121	18.8	**2.95**
116	9–11	**10**	3.54	127	19.7	**2.95**
116	9–11	**9.5**	3.72	134	20.8	**2.95**
116	9–11	**9**	3.93	142	22	**2.95**
117	9–11	**15**	2.34	84	13	**2.92**
117	9–11	**14.5**	2.42	87	13.5	**2.92**
117	9–11	**14**	2.51	90	14	**2.92**
117	9–11	**13.5**	2.6	94	14.6	**2.92**
117	9–11	**13**	2.7	97	15	**2.92**
117	9–11	**12.5**	2.81	101	15.7	**2.92**
117	9–11	**12**	2.92	105	16.3	**2.92**
117	9–11	**11.5**	3.05	110	17.1	**2.92**
117	9–11	**11**	3.19	115	17.8	**2.92**
117	9–11	**10.5**	3.34	120	18.6	**2.92**
117	9–11	**10**	3.51	126	19.5	**2.92**
117	9–11	**9.5**	3.69	133	20.6	**2.92**
117	9–11	**9**	3.9	140	21.7	**2.92**
118	9–11	**15**	2.32	83	12.9	**2.9**
118	9–11	**14.5**	2.4	86	13.3	**2.9**

A/L	Sizes	Body	1 sq.pi.	1 sq.in.	1 sq.cm.	Ch./pi.
118	9–11	14	2.48	89	13.8	2.9
118	9–11	13.5	2.58	93	14.4	2.9
118	9–11	13	2.68	96	14.9	2.9
118	9–11	12.5	2.78	100	15.5	2.9
118	9–11	12	2.9	104	16.1	2.9
118	9–11	11.5	3.02	109	16.9	2.9
118	9–11	11	3.16	114	17.7	2.9
118	9–11	10.5	3.31	119	18.4	2.9
118	9–11	10	3.48	125	19.4	2.9
118	9–11	9.5	3.66	132	20.5	2.9
118	9–11	9	3.86	139	21.5	2.9
119	9–11	15	2.3	83	12.9	2.87
119	9–11	14.5	2.38	86	13.3	2.87
119	9–11	14	2.46	89	13.8	2.87
119	9–11	13.5	2.55	92	14.3	2.87
119	9–11	13	2.65	96	14.9	2.87
119	9–11	12.5	2.76	99	15.3	2.87
119	9–11	12	2.87	103	16	2.87
119	9–11	11.5	3	108	16.7	2.87
119	9–11	11	3.14	113	17.5	2.87
119	9–11	10.5	3.28	118	18.3	2.87
119	9–11	10	3.45	124	19.2	2.87
119	9–11	9.5	3.63	131	20.3	2.87
119	9–11	9	3.83	138	21.4	2.87
120	9–12	16	2.14	77	11.9	2.85
120	9–12	15.5	2.21	79	12.2	2.85
120	9–12	15	2.28	82	12.7	2.85
120	9–12	14.5	2.36	85	13.2	2.85
120	9–12	14	2.44	88	13.6	2.85
120	9–12	13.5	2.53	91	14.1	2.85
120	9–12	13	2.63	95	14.7	2.85
120	9–12	12.5	2.74	98	15.2	2.85
120	9–12	12	2.85	103	16	2.85
120	9–12	11.5	2.97	107	16.6	2.85
120	9–12	11	3.11	112	17.4	2.85
120	9–12	10.5	3.26	117	18.1	2.85
120	9–12	10	3.42	123	19.1	2.85
120	9–12	9.5	3.6	130	20.2	2.85
120	9–12	9	3.8	137	21.2	2.85
121	9–12	16	2.12	76	11.8	2.83
121	9–12	15.5	2.19	79	12.2	2.83
121	9–12	15	2.26	81	12.6	2.83
121	9–12	14.5	2.34	84	13	2.83

A/L	Sizes	Body	1 sq.pi.	1 sq.in.	1 sq.cm.	Ch./pi.
121	9–12	14	2.42	87	13.5	2.83
121	9–12	13.5	2.51	90	14	2.83
121	9–12	13	2.61	94	14.6	2.83
121	9–12	12.5	2.71	98	15.2	2.83
121	9–12	12	2.83	102	15.8	2.83
121	9–12	11.5	2.95	106	16.4	2.83
121	9–12	11	3.08	111	17.2	2.83
121	9–12	10.5	3.23	116	18	2.83
121	9–12	10	3.39	122	18.9	2.83
121	9–12	9.5	2.57	129	20	2.83
121	9–12	9	3.77	136	21.1	2.83
122	9–12	16	2.1	76	11.8	2.8
122	9–12	15.5	2.17	78	12.1	2.8
122	9–12	15	2.24	81	12.6	2.8
122	9–12	14.5	2.32	84	13	2.8
122	9–12	14	2.4	87	13.5	2.8
122	9–12	13.5	2.49	90	14	2.8
122	9–12	13	2.59	93	14.4	2.8
122	9–12	12.5	2.69	97	15	2.8
122	9–12	12	2.8	101	15.7	2.8
122	9–12	11.5	2.93	105	16.3	2.8
122	9–12	11	3.06	110	17.1	2.8
122	9–12	10.5	3.2	115	17.8	2.8
122	9–12	10	3.36	121	18.8	2.8
122	9–12	9.5	3.54	127	19.7	2.8
122	9–12	9	3.74	135	20.9	2.8
123	9–12	16	2.09	75	11.6	2.78
123	9–12	15.5	2.15	77	11.9	2.78
123	9–12	15	2.22	80	12.4	2.78
123	9–12	14.5	2.3	83	12.9	2.78
123	9–12	14	2.38	86	13.3	2.78
123	9–12	13.5	2.47	89	13.8	2.78
123	9–12	13	2.57	92	14.3	2.78
123	9–12	12.5	2.67	96	14.9	2.78
123	9–12	12	2.78	100	15.5	2.78
123	9–12	11.5	2.9	104	16.1	2.78
123	9–12	11	3.03	109	16.9	2.78
123	9–12	10.5	3.18	114	17.7	2.78
123	9–12	10	3.34	120	18.6	2.78
123	9–12	9.5	3.51	126	19.5	2.78
123	9–12	9	3.71	133	20.6	2.78
124	9–12	16	2.07	74	11.5	2.76
124	9–12	15.5	2.14	77	11.9	2.76

A/L	Sizes	Body	1 sq.pi.	1 sq.in.	1 sq.cm.	Ch./pi.
124	9–12	15	2.21	79	12.2	2.76
124	9–12	14.5	2.28	82	12.7	2.76
124	9–12	14	2.36	85	13.2	2.76
124	9–12	13.5	2.45	88	13.6	2.76
124	9–12	13	2.55	92	14.3	2.76
124	9–12	12.5	2.65	95	14.7	2.76
124	9–12	12	2.76	99	15.3	2.76
124	9–12	11.5	2.88	104	16.1	2.76
124	9–12	11	3.01	108	16.7	2.76
124	9–12	10.5	3.15	113	17.5	2.76
124	9–12	10	3.31	119	18.4	2.76
124	9–12	9.5	3.48	125	19.4	2.76
124	9–12	9	3.68	132	20.5	2.76
125	9–12	16	2.05	74	11.5	2.74
125	9–12	15.5	2.12	76	11.8	2.74
125	9–12	15	2.19	79	12.2	2.74
125	9–12	14.5	2.26	82	12.7	2.74
125	9–12	14	2.35	84	13	2.74
125	9–12	13.5	2.43	88	13.6	2.74
125	9–12	13	2.53	91	14.1	2.74
125	9–12	12.5	2.63	95	14.7	2.74
125	9–12	12	2.74	98	15.2	2.74
125	9–12	11.5	2.85	103	16	2.74
125	9–12	11	2.98	107	16.6	2.74
125	9–12	10.5	3.13	113	17.5	2.74
125	9–12	10	3.28	118	18.3	2.74
125	9–12	9.5	3.46	124	19.2	2.74
125	9–12	9	3.65	131	20.3	2.74
126	9–12	16	2.04	73	11.3	2.71
126	9–12	15.5	2.1	76	11.8	2.71
126	9–12	15	2.17	78	12.1	2.71
126	9–12	14.5	2.25	81	12.6	2.71
126	9–12	14	2.33	84	13	2.71
126	9–12	13.5	2.41	87	13.5	2.71
126	9–12	13	2.51	90	14	2.71
126	9–12	12.5	2.61	94	14.6	2.71
126	9–12	12	2.71	98	15.2	2.71
126	9–12	11.5	2.83	102	15.8	2.71
126	9–12	11	2.96	107	16.6	2.71
126	9–12	10.5	3.1	112	17.4	2.71
126	9–12	10	3.26	117	18.1	2.71
126	9–12	9.5	3.43	123	19.1	2.71
126	9–12	9	3.62	130	20.2	2.71

A/L	Sizes	Body	1 sq.pi.	1 sq.in.	1 sq.cm.	Ch./pi.
127	10–13	**17**	1.9	68	10.5	**2.69**
127	10–13	**16.5**	1.96	71	11	**2.69**
127	10–13	**16**	2.02	73	11.3	**2.69**
127	10–13	**15.5**	2.08	75	11.6	**2.69**
127	10–13	**15**	2.15	78	12.1	**2.69**
127	10–13	**14.5**	2.23	80	12.4	**2.69**
127	10–13	**14**	2.31	83	12.9	**2.69**
127	10–13	**13.5**	2.39	86	13.3	**2.69**
127	10–13	**13**	2.49	89	13.8	**2.69**
127	10–13	**12.5**	2.59	93	14.4	**2.69**
127	10–13	**12**	2.69	97	15	**2.69**
127	10–13	**11.5**	2.81	101	15.7	**2.69**
127	10–13	**11**	2.94	106	16.4	**2.69**
127	10–13	**10.5**	3.08	111	17.2	**2.69**
127	10–13	**10**	3.23	116	18	**2.69**
128	10–13	**17**	1.89	68	10.5	**2.67**
128	10–13	**16.5**	1.94	70	10.9	**2.67**
128	10–13	**16**	2	72	11.2	**2.67**
128	10–13	**15.5**	2.07	74	11.5	**2.67**
128	10–13	**15**	2.14	77	11.9	**2.67**
128	10–13	**14.5**	2.21	80	12.4	**2.67**
128	10–13	**14**	2.29	82	12.7	**2.67**
128	10–13	**13.5**	2.37	85	13.2	**2.67**
128	10–13	**13**	2.47	89	13.8	**2.67**
128	10–13	**12.5**	2.57	92	14.3	**2.67**
128	10–13	**12**	2.67	96	14.9	**2.67**
128	10–13	**11.5**	2.79	100	15.5	**2.67**
128	10–13	**11**	2.91	105	16.3	**2.67**
128	10–13	**10.5**	3.05	110	17.1	**2.67**
128	10–13	**10**	3.21	115	17.8	**2.67**
129	10–13	**17**	1.87	67	10.4	**2.65**
129	10–13	**16.5**	1.93	69	10.7	**2.65**
129	10–13	**16**	1.99	72	11.2	**2.65**
129	10–13	**15.5**	2.05	74	11.5	**2.65**
129	10–13	**15**	2.12	76	11.8	**2.65**
129	10–13	**14.5**	2.19	79	12.2	**2.65**
129	10–13	**14**	2.27	82	12.7	**2.65**
129	10–13	**13.5**	2.36	85	13.2	**2.65**
129	10–13	**13**	2.45	88	13.6	**2.65**
129	10–13	**12.5**	2.55	92	14.3	**2.65**
129	10–13	**12**	2.65	95	14.7	**2.65**
129	10–13	**11.5**	2.77	100	15.5	**2.65**
129	10–13	**11**	2.89	104	16.1	**2.65**
129	10–13	**10.5**	3.03	109	16.9	**2.65**

A/L	Sizes	Body	1 sq.pi.	1 sq.in.	1 sq.cm.	Ch./pi.
129	10–13	**10**	3.18	115	17.8	**2.65**
130	10–13	**17**	1.86	67	10.4	**2.63**
130	10–13	**16.5**	1.91	69	10.7	**2.63**
130	10–13	**16**	1.97	71	11	**2.63**
130	10–13	**15.5**	2.04	73	11.3	**2.63**
130	10–13	**15**	2.1	76	11.8	**2.63**
130	10–13	**14.5**	2.18	78	12.1	**2.63**
130	10–13	**14**	2.25	81	12.6	**2.63**
130	10–13	**13.5**	2.34	84	13	**2.63**
130	10–13	**13**	2.43	87	13.5	**2.63**
130	10–13	**12.5**	2.53	91	14.1	**2.63**
130	10–13	**12**	2.63	95	14.7	**2.63**
130	10–13	**11.5**	2.75	99	15.3	**2.63**
130	10–13	**11**	2.87	103	16	**2.63**
130	10–13	**10.5**	3.01	108	16.7	**2.63**
130	10–13	**10**	3.16	114	17.7	**2.63**
131	10–13	**17**	1.84	66	10.2	**2.61**
131	10–13	**16.5**	1.9	68	10.5	**2.61**
131	10–13	**16**	1.96	70	10.9	**2.61**
131	10–13	**15.5**	2.02	73	11.3	**2.61**
131	10–13	**15**	2.09	75	11.6	**2.61**
131	10–13	**14.5**	2.16	78	12.1	**2.61**
131	10–13	**14**	2.24	81	12.6	**2.61**
131	10–13	**13.5**	2.32	84	13	**2.61**
131	10–13	**13**	2.41	87	13.5	**2.61**
131	10–13	**12.5**	2.51	90	14	**2.61**
131	10–13	**12**	2.61	94	14.6	**2.61**
131	10–13	**11.5**	2.72	98	15.2	**2.61**
131	10–13	**11**	2.85	103	16	**2.61**
131	10–13	**10.5**	2.98	107	16.6	**2.61**
131	10–13	**10**	3.13	113	17.5	**2.61**
132	10–13	**17**	1.83	66	10.2	**2.59**
132	10–13	**16.5**	1.88	68	10.5	**2.59**
132	10–13	**16**	1.94	70	10.9	**2.59**
132	10–13	**15.5**	2.01	72	11.2	**2.59**
132	10–13	**15**	2.07	75	11.6	**2.59**
132	10–13	**14.5**	2.14	77	11.9	**2.59**
132	10–13	**14**	2.22	80	12.4	**2.59**
132	10–13	**13.5**	2.3	83	12.9	**2.59**
132	10–13	**13**	2.39	86	13.3	**2.59**
132	10–13	**12.5**	2.49	90	14	**2.59**
132	10–13	**12**	2.59	93	14.4	**2.59**
132	10–13	**11.5**	2.7	97	15	**2.59**

A/L	Sizes	Body	1 sq.pi.	1 sq.in.	1 sq.cm.	Ch./pi.
132	10–13	**11**	2.83	102	15.8	**2.59**
132	10–13	**10.5**	2.96	107	16.6	**2.59**
132	10–13	**10**	3.11	112	17.4	**2.59**
133	10–13	**17**	1.82	65	10.1	**2.57**
133	10–13	**16.5**	1.87	67	10.4	**2.57**
133	10–13	**16**	1.93	69	10.7	**2.57**
133	10–13	**15.5**	1.99	72	11.2	**2.57**
133	10–13	**15**	2.06	74	11.5	**2.57**
133	10–13	**14.5**	2.13	77	11.9	**2.57**
133	10–13	**14**	2.2	79	12.2	**2.57**
133	10–13	**13.5**	2.29	82	12.7	**2.57**
133	10–13	**13**	2.37	85	13.2	**2.57**
133	10–13	**12.5**	2.47	89	13.8	**2.57**
133	10–13	**12**	2.57	93	14.4	**2.57**
133	10–13	**11.5**	2.68	97	15	**2.57**
133	10–13	**11**	2.81	101	15.7	**2.57**
133	10–13	**10.5**	2.94	106	16.4	**2.57**
133	10–13	**10**	3.09	111	17.2	**2.57**
134	10–13	**17**	1.8	65	10.1	**2.55**
134	10–13	**16.5**	1.86	67	10.4	**2.55**
134	10–13	**16**	1.91	69	10.7	**2.55**
134	10–13	**15.5**	1.98	71	11	**2.55**
134	10–13	**15**	2.04	74	11.5	**2.55**
134	10–13	**14.5**	2.11	76	11.8	**2.55**
134	10–13	**14**	2.19	79	12.2	**2.55**
134	10–13	**13.5**	2.27	82	12.7	**2.55**
134	10–13	**13**	2.36	85	13.2	**2.55**
134	10–13	**12.5**	2.45	88	13.6	**2.55**
134	10–13	**12**	2.55	92	14.3	**2.55**
134	10–13	**11.5**	2.66	96	14.9	**2.55**
134	10–13	**11**	2.78	100	15.5	**2.55**
134	10–13	**10.5**	2.92	105	16.3	**2.55**
134	10–13	**10**	3.06	110	17.1	**2.55**
135	10–13	**17**	1.79	64	9.9	**2.53**
135	10–13	**16.5**	1.84	66	10.2	**2.53**
135	10–13	**16**	1.9	68	10.5	**2.53**
135	10–13	**15.5**	1.96	71	11	**2.53**
135	10–13	**15**	2.03	73	11.3	**2.53**
135	10–13	**14.5**	2.1	75	11.6	**2.53**
135	10–13	**14**	2.17	78	12.1	**2.53**
135	10–13	**13.5**	2.25	81	12.6	**2.53**
135	10–13	**13**	2.34	84	13	**2.53**
135	10–13	**12.5**	2.43	88	13.6	**2.53**

A/L	Sizes	Body	1 sq.pi.	1 sq.in.	1 sq.cm.	Ch./pi.
135	10–13	12	2.53	91	14.1	2.53
135	10–13	11.5	2.64	95	14.7	2.53
135	10–13	11	2.76	99	15.3	2.53
135	10–13	10.5	2.9	104	16.1	2.53
135	10–13	10	3.04	109	16.9	2.53
136	10–13	17	1.78	64	9.9	2.51
136	10–13	16.5	1.83	66	10.2	2.51
136	10–13	16	1.89	68	10.5	2.51
136	10–13	15.5	1.95	70	10.9	2.51
136	10–13	15	2.01	72	11.2	2.51
136	10–13	14.5	2.08	75	11.6	2.51
136	10–13	14	2.16	78	12.1	2.51
136	10–13	13.5	2.24	80	12.4	2.51
136	10–13	13	2.32	84	13	2.51
136	10–13	12.5	2.41	87	13.5	2.51
136	10–13	12	2.51	91	14.1	2.51
136	10–13	11.5	2.62	94	14.6	2.51
136	10–13	11	2.74	99	15.3	2.51
136	10–13	10.5	2.87	103	16	2.51
136	10–13	10	3.02	109	16.9	2.51
137	10–14	18	1.66	60	9.3	2.5
137	10–14	17.5	1.71	62	9.6	2.5
137	10–14	17	1.76	63	9.8	2.5
137	10–14	16.5	1.82	65	10.1	2.5
137	10–14	16	1.87	67	10.4	2.5
137	10–14	15.5	1.93	70	10.9	2.5
137	10–14	15	2	72	11.2	2.5
137	10–14	14.5	2.07	74	11.5	2.5
137	10–14	14	2.14	77	11.9	2.5
137	10–14	13.5	2.22	80	12.4	2.5
137	10–14	13	2.3	83	12.9	2.5
137	10–14	12.5	2.4	86	13.3	2.5
137	10–14	12	2.5	90	14	2.5
137	10–14	11.5	2.6	94	14.6	2.5
137	10–14	11	2.72	98	15.2	2.5
137	10–14	10.5	2.85	103	16	2.5
137	10–14	10	3	108	16.7	2.5
138	10–14	18	1.65	59	9.1	2.48
138	10–14	17.5	1.7	61	9.5	2.48
138	10–14	17	1.75	63	9.8	2.48
138	10–14	16.5	1.8	65	10.1	2.48
138	10–14	16	1.86	67	10.4	2.48
138	10–14	15.5	1.92	69	10.7	2.48

A/L	Sizes	Body	1 sq.pi.	1 sq.in.	1 sq.cm.	Ch./pi.
138	10–14	15	1.98	71	11	2.48
138	10–14	14.5	2.05	74	11.5	2.48
138	10–14	14	2.12	76	11.8	2.48
138	10–14	13.5	2.2	79	12.2	2.48
138	10–14	13	2.29	82	12.7	2.48
138	10–14	12.5	2.38	86	13.3	2.48
138	10–14	12	2.48	89	13.8	2.48
138	10–14	11.5	2.59	93	14.4	2.48
138	10–14	11	2.7	97	15	2.48
138	10–14	10.5	2.83	102	15.8	2.48
138	10–14	10	2.97	107	16.6	2.48
139	10–14	18	1.64	59	9.1	2.46
139	10–14	17.5	1.69	61	9.5	2.46
139	10–14	17	1.74	63	9.8	2.46
139	10–14	16.5	1.79	64	9.9	2.46
139	10–14	16	1.85	66	10.2	2.46
139	10–14	15.5	1.9	69	10.7	2.46
139	10–14	15	1.97	71	11	2.46
139	10–14	14.5	2.04	73	11.3	2.46
139	10–14	14	2.11	76	11.8	2.46
139	10–14	13.5	2.19	79	12.2	2.46
139	10–14	13	2.27	82	12.7	2.46
139	10–14	12.5	2.36	85	13.2	2.46
139	10–14	12	2.46	89	13.8	2.46
139	10–14	11.5	2.57	92	14.3	2.46
139	10–14	11	2.68	97	15	2.46
139	10–14	10.5	2.81	101	15.7	2.46
139	10–14	10	2.95	106	16.4	2.46
140	10–14	18	1.63	59	9.1	2.44
140	10–14	17.5	1.68	60	9.3	2.44
140	10–14	17	1.72	62	9.6	2.44
140	10–14	16.5	1.78	64	9.9	2.44
140	10–14	16	1.83	66	10.2	2.44
140	10–14	15.5	1.89	68	10.5	2.44
140	10–14	15	1.95	70	10.9	2.44
140	10–14	14.5	2.02	73	11.3	2.44
140	10–14	14	2.09	75	11.6	2.44
140	10–14	13.5	2.17	78	12.1	2.44
140	10–14	13	2.25	81	12.6	2.44
140	10–14	12.5	2.35	84	13	2.44
140	10–14	12	2.44	88	13.6	2.44
140	10–14	11.5	2.55	92	14.3	2.44
140	10–14	11	2.66	96	14.9	2.44
140	10–14	10.5	2.79	101	15.7	2.44

A/L	Sizes	Body	1 sq.pi.	1 sq.in.	1 sq.cm.	Ch./pi.
140	10–14	**10**	2.93	106	16.4	**2.44**
141	10–14	**18**	1.62	58	9	**2.43**
141	10–14	**17.5**	1.66	60	9.3	**2.43**
141	10–14	**17**	1.71	62	9.6	**2.43**
141	10–14	**16.5**	1.76	64	9.9	**2.43**
141	10–14	**16**	1.82	65	10.1	**2.43**
141	10–14	**15.5**	1.88	68	10.5	**2.43**
141	10–14	**15**	1.94	70	10.9	**2.43**
141	10–14	**14.5**	2.01	72	11.2	**2.43**
141	10–14	**14**	2.08	75	11.6	**2.43**
141	10–14	**13.5**	2.16	78	12.1	**2.43**
141	10–14	**13**	2.24	81	12.6	**2.43**
141	10–14	**12.5**	2.33	84	13	**2.43**
141	10–14	**12**	2.43	87	13.5	**2.43**
141	10–14	**11.5**	2.53	91	14.1	**2.43**
141	10–14	**11**	2.65	95	14.7	**2.43**
141	10–14	**10.5**	2.77	100	15.5	**2.43**
141	10–14	**10**	2.91	105	16.3	**2.43**
142	11–14	**18**	1.61	58	9	**2.41**
142	11–14	**17.5**	1.65	59	9.1	**2.41**
142	11–14	**17**	1.7	61	9.5	**2.41**
142	11–14	**16.5**	1.75	63	9.8	**2.41**
142	11–14	**16**	1.81	65	10.1	**2.41**
142	11–14	**15.5**	1.86	67	10.4	**2.41**
142	11–14	**15**	1.93	69	10.7	**2.41**
142	11–14	**14.5**	1.99	72	11.2	**2.41**
142	11–14	**14**	2.06	74	11.5	**2.41**
142	11–14	**13.5**	2.14	77	11.9	**2.41**
142	11–14	**13**	2.22	80	12.4	**2.41**
142	11–14	**12.5**	2.31	83	12.9	**2.41**
142	11–14	**12**	2.41	87	13.5	**2.41**
142	11–14	**11.5**	2.51	90	14	**2.41**
142	11–14	**11**	2.63	95	14.7	**2.41**
143	11–14	**18**	1.59	57	8.8	**2.39**
143	11–14	**17.5**	1.64	59	9.1	**2.39**
143	11–14	**17**	1.69	61	9.5	**2.39**
143	11–14	**16.5**	1.74	63	9.8	**2.39**
143	11–14	**16**	1.79	65	10.1	**2.39**
143	11–14	**15.5**	1.85	67	10.4	**2.39**
143	11–14	**15**	1.91	69	10.7	**2.39**
143	11–14	**14.5**	1.98	71	11	**2.39**
143	11–14	**14**	2.05	74	11.5	**2.39**
143	11–14	**13.5**	2.13	77	11.9	**2.39**

A/L	Sizes	Body	1 sq.pi.	1 sq.in.	1 sq.cm.	Ch./pi.
143	11–14	13	2.21	79	12.2	2.39
143	11–14	12.5	2.3	83	12.9	2.39
143	11–14	12	2.39	86	13.3	2.39
143	11–14	11.5	2.5	90	14	2.39
143	11–14	11	2.61	94	14.6	2.39
144	11–14	18	1.58	57	8.8	2.38
144	11–14	17.5	1.63	59	9.1	2.38
144	11–14	17	1.68	60	9.3	2.38
144	11–14	16.5	1.73	62	9.6	2.38
144	11–14	16	1.78	64	9.9	2.38
144	11–14	15.5	1.84	66	10.2	2.38
144	11–14	15	1.9	68	10.5	2.38
144	11–14	14.5	1.97	71	11	2.38
144	11–14	14	2.04	73	11.3	2.38
144	11–14	13.5	2.11	76	11.8	2.38
144	11–14	13	2.19	79	12.2	2.38
144	11–14	12.5	2.28	82	12.7	2.38
144	11–14	12	2.38	86	13.3	2.38
144	11–14	11.5	2.48	89	13.8	2.38
144	11–14	11	2.59	93	14.4	2.38
145	11–15	19	1.49	54	8.4	2.36
145	11–15	18.5	1.53	55	8.5	2.36
145	11–15	18	1.57	57	8.8	2.36
145	11–15	17.5	1.62	58	9	2.36
145	11–15	17	1.66	60	9.3	2.36
145	11–15	16.5	1.72	62	9.6	2.36
145	11–15	16	1.77	64	9.9	2.36
145	11–15	15.5	1.83	66	10.2	2.36
145	11–15	15	1.89	68	10.5	2.36
145	11–15	14.5	1.95	70	10.9	2.36
145	11–15	14	2.02	73	11.3	2.36
145	11–15	13.5	2.1	75	11.6	2.36
145	11–15	13	2.18	78	12.1	2.36
145	11–15	12.5	2.26	82	12.7	2.36
145	11–15	12	2.36	85	13.2	2.36
145	11–15	11.5	2.46	89	13.8	2.36
145	11–15	11	2.57	93	14.4	2.36
146	11–15	19	1.48	53	8.2	2.34
146	11–15	18.5	1.52	55	8.5	2.34
146	11–15	18	1.56	56	8.7	2.34
146	11–15	17.5	1.61	58	9	2.34
146	11–15	17	1.65	60	9.3	2.34
146	11–15	16.5	1.7	61	9.5	2.34

A/L	Sizes	Body	1 sq.pi.	1 sq.in.	1 sq.cm.	Ch./pi.
146	11–15	**16**	1.76	63	9.8	**2.34**
146	11–15	**15.5**	1.81	65	10.1	**2.34**
146	11–15	**15**	1.87	67	10.4	**2.34**
146	11–15	**14.5**	1.94	70	10.9	**2.34**
146	11–15	**14**	2.01	72	11.2	**2.34**
146	11–15	**13.5**	2.08	75	11.6	**2.34**
146	11–15	**13**	2.16	78	12.1	**2.34**
146	11–15	**12.5**	2.25	81	12.6	**2.34**
146	11–15	**12**	2.34	84	13	**2.34**
146	11–15	**11.5**	2.44	88	13.6	**2.34**
146	11–15	**11**	2.56	92	14.3	**2.34**
147	11–15	**19**	1.47	53	8.2	**2.33**
147	11–15	**18.5**	1.51	54	8.4	**2.33**
147	11–15	**18**	1.55	56	8.7	**2.33**
147	11–15	**17.5**	1.6	57	8.8	**2.33**
147	11–15	**17**	1.64	59	9.1	**2.33**
147	11–15	**16.5**	1.69	61	9.5	**2.33**
147	11–15	**16**	1.74	63	9.8	**2.33**
147	11–15	**15.5**	1.8	65	10.1	**2.33**
147	11–15	**15**	1.86	67	10.4	**2.33**
147	11–15	**14.5**	1.93	69	10.7	**2.33**
147	11–15	**14**	1.99	72	11.2	**2.33**
147	11–15	**13.5**	2.07	74	11.5	**2.33**
147	11–15	**13**	2.15	77	11.9	**2.33**
147	11–15	**12.5**	2.23	80	12.4	**2.33**
147	11–15	**12**	2.33	84	13	**2.33**
147	11–15	**11.5**	2.43	87	13.5	**2.33**
147	11–15	**11**	2.54	91	14.1	**2.33**
148	11–15	**19**	1.46	53	8.2	**2.31**
148	11–15	**18.5**	1.5	54	8.4	**2.31**
148	11–15	**18**	1.54	55	8.5	**2.31**
148	11–15	**17.5**	1.58	57	8.8	**2.31**
148	11–15	**17**	1.63	59	9.1	**2.31**
148	11–15	**16.5**	1.68	61	9.5	**2.31**
148	11–15	**16**	1.73	62	9.6	**2.31**
148	11–15	**15.5**	1.79	64	9.9	**2.31**
148	11–15	**15**	1.85	67	10.4	**2.31**
148	11–15	**14.5**	1.91	69	10.7	**2.31**
148	11–15	**14**	1.98	71	11	**2.31**
148	11–15	**13.5**	2.05	74	11.5	**2.31**
148	11–15	**13**	2.13	77	11.9	**2.31**
148	11–15	**12.5**	2.22	80	12.4	**2.31**
148	11–15	**12**	2.31	83	12.9	**2.31**
148	11–15	**11.5**	2.41	87	13.5	**2.31**

A/L	Sizes	Body	1 sq.pi.	1 sq.in.	1 sq.cm.	Ch./pi.
148	11–15	**11**	2.52	91	14.1	**2.31**
149	11–15	**19**	1.45	52	8.1	**2.3**
149	11–15	**18.5**	1.49	54	8.4	**2.3**
149	11–15	**18**	1.53	55	8.5	**2.3**
149	11–15	**17.5**	1.57	57	8.8	**2.3**
149	11–15	**17**	1.62	58	9	**2.3**
149	11–15	**16.5**	1.67	60	9.3	**2.3**
149	11–15	**16**	1.72	62	9.6	**2.3**
149	11–15	**15.5**	1.78	64	9.9	**2.3**
149	11–15	**15**	1.84	66	10.2	**2.3**
149	11–15	**14.5**	1.9	68	10.5	**2.3**
149	11–15	**14**	1.97	71	11	**2.3**
149	11–15	**13.5**	2.04	73	11.3	**2.3**
149	11–15	**13**	2.12	76	11.8	**2.3**
149	11–15	**12.5**	2.2	79	12.2	**2.3**
149	11–15	**12**	2.3	83	12.9	**2.3**
149	11–15	**11.5**	2.4	86	13.3	**2.3**
149	11–15	**11**	2.5	90	14	**2.3**
150	11–15	**19**	1.44	52	8.1	**2.28**
150	11–15	**18.5**	1.48	53	8.2	**2.28**
150	11–15	**18**	1.52	55	8.5	**2.28**
150	11–15	**17.5**	1.56	56	8.7	**2.28**
150	11–15	**17**	1.61	58	9	**2.28**
150	11–15	**16.5**	1.66	60	9.3	**2.28**
150	11–15	**16**	1.71	62	9.6	**2.28**
150	11–15	**15.5**	1.77	64	9.9	**2.28**
150	11–15	**15**	1.82	66	10.2	**2.28**
150	11–15	**14.5**	1.89	68	10.5	**2.28**
150	11–15	**14**	1.95	70	10.9	**2.28**
150	11–15	**13.5**	2.03	73	11.3	**2.28**
150	11–15	**13**	2.1	76	11.8	**2.28**
150	11–15	**12.5**	2.19	79	12.2	**2.28**
150	11–15	**12**	2.28	82	12.7	**2.28**
150	11–15	**11.5**	2.38	86	13.3	**2.28**
150	11–15	**11**	2.49	90	14	**2.28**
151	11–15	**19**	1.43	51	7.9	**2.26**
151	11–15	**18.5**	1.47	53	8.2	**2.26**
151	11–15	**18**	1.51	54	8.4	**2.26**
151	11–15	**17.5**	1.55	56	8.7	**2.26**
151	11–15	**17**	1.6	58	9	**2.26**
151	11–15	**16.5**	1.65	59	9.1	**2.26**
151	11–15	**16**	1.7	61	9.5	**2.26**
151	11–15	**15.5**	1.75	63	9.8	**2.26**

A/L	Sizes	Body	1 sq.pi.	1 sq.in.	1 sq.cm.	Ch./pi.
151	11–15	15	1.81	65	10.1	2.26
151	11–15	14.5	1.87	67	10.4	2.26
151	11–15	14	1.94	70	10.9	2.26
151	11–15	13.5	2.01	72	11.2	2.26
151	11–15	13	2.09	75	11.6	2.26
151	11–15	12.5	2.17	78	12.1	2.26
151	11–15	12	2.26	82	12.7	2.26
151	11–15	11.5	2.36	85	13.2	2.26
151	11–15	11	2.47	89	13.8	2.26
152	11–15	19	1.42	51	7.9	2.25
152	11–15	18.5	1.46	53	8.2	2.25
152	11–15	18	1.5	54	8.4	2.25
152	11–15	17.5	1.54	56	8.7	2.25
152	11–15	17	1.59	57	8.8	2.25
152	11–15	16.5	1.64	59	9.1	2.25
152	11–15	16	1.69	61	9.5	2.25
152	11–15	15.5	1.74	63	9.8	2.25
152	11–15	15	1.8	65	10.1	2.25
152	11–15	14.5	1.86	67	10.4	2.25
152	11–15	14	1.93	69	10.7	2.25
152	11–15	13.5	2	72	11.2	2.25
152	11–15	13	2.08	75	11.6	2.25
152	11–15	12.5	2.16	78	12.1	2.25
152	11–15	12	2.25	81	12.6	2.25
152	11–15	11.5	2.35	85	13.2	2.25
152	11–15	11	2.45	88	13.6	2.25
153	11–16	20	1.34	48	7.4	2.24
153	11–16	19.5	1.38	50	7.8	2.24
153	11–16	19	1.41	51	7.9	2.24
153	11–16	18.5	1.45	52	8.1	2.24
153	11–16	18	1.49	54	8.4	2.24
153	11–16	17.5	1.53	55	8.5	2.24
153	11–16	17	1.58	57	8.8	2.24
153	11–16	16.5	1.63	59	9.1	2.24
153	11–16	16	1.68	60	9.3	2.24
153	11–16	15.5	1.73	62	9.6	2.24
153	11–16	15	1.79	64	9.9	2.24
153	11–16	14.5	1.85	67	10.4	2.24
153	11–16	14	1.92	69	10.7	2.24
153	11–16	13.5	1.99	72	11.2	2.24
153	11–16	13	2.06	74	11.5	2.24
153	11–16	12.5	2.15	77	11.9	2.24
153	11–16	12	2.24	80	12.4	2.24
153	11–16	11.5	2.33	84	13	2.24

A/L	Sizes	Body	1 sq.pi.	1 sq.in.	1 sq.cm.	Ch./pi.
153	11–16	**11**	2.44	88	13.6	**2.24**
154	11–16	**20**	1.33	48	7.4	**2.22**
154	11–16	**19.5**	1.37	49	7.6	**2.22**
154	11–16	**19**	1.4	50	7.8	**2.22**
154	11–16	**18.5**	1.44	52	8.1	**2.22**
154	11–16	**18**	1.48	53	8.2	**2.22**
154	11–16	**17.5**	1.52	55	8.5	**2.22**
154	11–16	**17**	1.57	56	8.7	**2.22**
154	11–16	**16.5**	1.62	58	9	**2.22**
154	11–16	**16**	1.67	60	9.3	**2.22**
154	11–16	**15.5**	1.72	62	9.6	**2.22**
154	11–16	**15**	1.78	64	9.9	**2.22**
154	11–16	**14.5**	1.84	66	10.2	**2.22**
154	11–16	**14**	1.9	69	10.7	**2.22**
154	11–16	**13.5**	1.97	71	11	**2.22**
154	11–16	**13**	2.05	74	11.5	**2.22**
154	11–16	**12.5**	2.13	77	11.9	**2.22**
154	11–16	**12**	2.22	80	12.4	**2.22**
154	11–16	**11.5**	2.32	83	12.9	**2.22**
154	11–16	**11**	2.42	87	13.5	**2.22**
155	11–16	**20**	1.32	48	7.4	**2.21**
155	11–16	**19.5**	1.36	49	7.6	**2.21**
155	11–16	**19**	1.39	50	7.8	**2.21**
155	11–16	**18.5**	1.43	52	8.1	**2.21**
155	11–16	**18**	1.47	53	8.2	**2.21**
155	11–16	**17.5**	1.51	54	8.4	**2.21**
155	11–16	**17**	1.56	56	8.7	**2.21**
155	11–16	**16.5**	1.6	58	9	**2.21**
155	11–16	**16**	1.65	60	9.3	**2.21**
155	11–16	**15.5**	1.71	61	9.5	**2.21**
155	11–16	**15**	1.77	64	9.9	**2.21**
155	11–16	**14.5**	1.83	66	10.2	**2.21**
155	11–16	**14**	1.89	68	10.5	**2.21**
155	11–16	**13.5**	1.96	71	11	**2.21**
155	11–16	**13**	2.04	73	11.3	**2.21**
155	11–16	**12.5**	2.12	76	11.8	**2.21**
155	11–16	**12**	2.21	79	12.2	**2.21**
155	11–16	**11.5**	2.3	83	12.9	**2.21**
155	11–16	**11**	2.41	87	13.5	**2.21**
156	12–16	**20**	1.32	47	7.3	**2.19**
156	12–16	**19.5**	1.35	49	7.6	**2.19**
156	12–16	**19**	1.38	50	7.8	**2.19**
156	12–16	**18.5**	1.42	51	7.9	**2.19**

A/L	Sizes	Body	1 sq.pi.	1 sq.in.	1 sq.cm.	Ch./pi.
156	12–16	18	1.46	53	8.2	2.19
156	12–16	17.5	1.5	54	8.4	2.19
156	12–16	17	1.55	56	8.7	2.19
156	12–16	16.5	1.59	57	8.8	2.19
156	12–16	16	1.64	59	9.1	2.19
156	12–16	15.5	1.7	61	9.5	2.19
156	12–16	15	1.75	63	9.8	2.19
156	12–16	14.5	1.81	65	10.1	2.19
156	12–16	14	1.88	68	10.5	2.19
156	12–16	13.5	1.95	70	10.9	2.19
156	12–16	13	2.02	73	11.3	2.19
156	12–16	12.5	2.1	76	11.8	2.19
156	12–16	12	2.19	79	12.2	2.19
157	12–16	20	1.31	47	7.3	2.18
157	12–16	19.5	1.34	48	7.4	2.18
157	12–16	19	1.38	50	7.8	2.18
157	12–16	18.5	1.41	51	7.9	2.18
157	12–16	18	1.45	52	8.1	2.18
157	12–16	17.5	1.49	54	8.4	2.18
157	12–16	17	1.54	55	8.5	2.18
157	12–16	16.5	1.58	57	8.8	2.18
157	12–16	16	1.63	59	9.1	2.18
157	12–16	15.5	1.69	61	9.5	2.18
157	12–16	15	1.74	63	9.8	2.18
157	12–16	14.5	1.8	65	10.1	2.18
157	12–16	14	1.87	67	10.4	2.18
157	12–16	13.5	1.94	70	10.9	2.18
157	12–16	13	2.01	72	11.2	2.18
157	12–16	12.5	2.09	75	11.6	2.18
157	12–16	12	2.18	78	12.1	2.18
158	12–16	20	1.3	47	7.3	2.16
158	12–16	19.5	1.33	48	7.4	2.16
158	12–16	19	1.37	49	7.6	2.16
158	12–16	18.5	1.4	51	7.9	2.16
158	12–16	18	1.44	52	8.1	2.16
158	12–16	17.5	1.48	53	8.2	2.16
158	12–16	17	1.53	55	8.5	2.16
158	12–16	16.5	1.57	57	8.8	2.16
158	12–16	16	1.62	58	9	2.16
158	12–16	15.5	1.68	60	9.3	2.16
158	12–16	15	1.73	62	9.6	2.16
158	12–16	14.5	1.79	64	9.9	2.16
158	12–16	14	1.86	67	10.4	2.16
158	12–16	13.5	1.92	69	10.7	2.16

A/L	Sizes	Body	1 sq.pi.	1 sq.in.	1 sq.cm.	Ch./pi.
158	12–16	**13**	2	72	11.2	**2.16**
158	12–16	**12.5**	2.08	75	11.6	**2.16**
158	12–16	**12**	2.16	78	12.1	**2.16**
159	12–16	**20**	1.29	46	7.1	**2.15**
159	12–16	**19.5**	1.32	48	7.4	**2.15**
159	12–16	**19**	1.36	49	7.6	**2.15**
159	12–16	**18.5**	1.4	50	7.8	**2.15**
159	12–16	**18**	1.43	52	8.1	**2.15**
159	12–16	**17.5**	1.47	53	8.2	**2.15**
159	12–16	**17**	1.52	55	8.5	**2.15**
159	12–16	**16.5**	1.56	56	8.7	**2.15**
159	12–16	**16**	1.61	58	9	**2.15**
159	12–16	**15.5**	1.67	60	9.3	**2.15**
159	12–16	**15**	1.72	62	9.6	**2.15**
159	12–16	**14.5**	1.78	64	9.9	**2.15**
159	12–16	**14**	1.84	66	10.2	**2.15**
159	12–16	**13.5**	1.91	69	10.7	**2.15**
159	12–16	**13**	1.99	71	11	**2.15**
159	12–16	**12.5**	2.06	74	11.5	**2.15**
159	12–16	**12**	2.15	77	11.9	**2.15**
160	12–16	**20**	1.28	46	7.1	**2.14**
160	12–16	**19.5**	1.32	47	7.3	**2.14**
160	12–16	**19**	1.35	49	7.6	**2.14**
160	12–16	**18.5**	1.39	50	7.8	**2.14**
160	12–16	**18**	1.43	51	7.9	**2.14**
160	12–16	**17.5**	1.47	53	8.2	**2.14**
160	12–16	**17**	1.51	54	8.4	**2.14**
160	12–16	**16.5**	1.55	56	8.7	**2.14**
160	12–16	**16**	1.6	58	9	**2.14**
160	12–16	**15.5**	1.65	60	9.3	**2.14**
160	12–16	**15**	1.71	62	9.6	**2.14**
160	12–16	**14.5**	1.77	64	9.9	**2.14**
160	12–16	**14**	1.83	66	10.2	**2.14**
160	12–16	**13.5**	1.9	68	10.5	**2.14**
160	12–16	**13**	1.97	71	11	**2.14**
160	12–16	**12.5**	2.05	74	11.5	**2.14**
160	12–16	**12**	2.14	77	11.9	**2.14**
161	12–16	**20**	1.27	46	7.1	**2.12**
161	12–16	**19.5**	1.31	47	7.3	**2.12**
161	12–16	**19**	1.34	48	7.4	**2.12**
161	12–16	**18.5**	1.38	50	7.8	**2.12**
161	12–16	**18**	1.42	51	7.9	**2.12**
161	12–16	**17.5**	1.46	52	8.1	**2.12**

A/L	Sizes	Body	1 sq.pi.	1 sq.in.	1 sq.cm.	Ch./pi.
161	12–16	17	1.5	54	8.4	2.12
161	12–16	16.5	1.54	56	8.7	2.12
161	12–16	16	1.59	57	8.8	2.12
161	12–16	15.5	1.64	59	9.1	2.12
161	12–16	15	1.7	61	9.5	2.12
161	12–16	14.5	1.76	63	9.8	2.12
161	12–16	14	1.82	66	10.2	2.12
161	12–16	13.5	1.89	68	10.5	2.12
161	12–16	13	1.96	71	11	2.12
161	12–16	12.5	2.04	73	11.3	2.12
161	12–16	12	2.12	76	11.8	2.12
162	12–16	20	1.27	46	7.1	2.11
162	12–16	19.5	1.3	47	7.3	2.11
162	12–16	19	1.33	48	7.4	2.11
162	12–16	18.5	1.37	49	7.6	2.11
162	12–16	18	1.41	51	7.9	2.11
162	12–16	17.5	1.45	52	8.1	2.11
162	12–16	17	1.49	54	8.4	2.11
162	12–16	16.5	1.54	55	8.5	2.11
162	12–16	16	1.58	57	8.8	2.11
162	12–16	15.5	1.63	59	9.1	2.11
162	12–16	15	1.69	61	9.5	2.11
162	12–16	14.5	1.75	63	9.8	2.11
162	12–16	14	1.81	65	10.1	2.11
162	12–16	13.5	1.88	68	10.5	2.11
162	12–16	13	1.95	70	10.9	2.11
162	12–16	12.5	2.03	73	11.3	2.11
162	12–16	12	2.11	76	11.8	2.11
163	12–17	21	1.2	43	6.7	2.1
163	12–17	20.5	1.23	44	6.8	2.1
163	12–17	20	1.26	45	7	2.1
163	12–17	19.5	1.29	46	7.1	2.1
163	12–17	19	1.33	48	7.4	2.1
163	12–17	18.5	1.36	49	7.6	2.1
163	12–17	18	1.4	50	7.8	2.1
163	12–17	17.5	1.44	52	8.1	2.1
163	12–17	17	1.48	53	8.2	2.1
163	12–17	16.5	1.53	55	8.5	2.1
163	12–17	16	1.57	57	8.8	2.1
163	12–17	15.5	1.62	58	9	2.1
163	12–17	15	1.68	60	9.3	2.1
163	12–17	14.5	1.74	63	9.8	2.1
163	12–17	14	1.8	65	10.1	2.1
163	12–17	13.5	1.87	67	10.4	2.1

A/L	Sizes	Body	1 sq.pi.	1 sq.in.	1 sq.cm.	Ch./pi.
163	12–17	**13**	1.94	70	10.9	**2.1**
163	12–17	**12.5**	2.01	73	11.3	**2.1**
163	12–17	**12**	2.1	76	11.8	**2.1**
164	12–17	**21**	1.19	43	6.7	**2.09**
164	12–17	**20.5**	1.22	44	6.8	**2.09**
164	12–17	**20**	1.25	45	7	**2.09**
164	12–17	**19.5**	1.28	46	7.1	**2.09**
164	12–17	**19**	1.32	47	7.3	**2.09**
164	12–17	**18.5**	1.35	49	7.6	**2.09**
164	12–17	**18**	1.39	50	7.8	**2.09**
164	12–17	**17.5**	1.43	51	7.9	**2.09**
164	12–17	**17**	1.47	53	8.2	**2.09**
164	12–17	**16.5**	1.52	55	8.5	**2.09**
164	12–17	**16**	1.56	56	8.7	**2.09**
164	12–17	**15.5**	1.61	58	9	**2.09**
164	12–17	**15**	1.67	60	9.3	**2.09**
164	12–17	**14.5**	1.73	62	9.6	**2.09**
164	12–17	**14**	1.79	64	9.9	**2.09**
164	12–17	**13.5**	1.85	67	10.4	**2.09**
164	12–17	**13**	1.92	69	10.7	**2.09**
164	12–17	**12.5**	2	72	11.2	**2.09**
164	12–17	**12**	2.09	75	11.6	**2.09**
165	12–17	**21**	1.18	43	6.7	**2.07**
165	12–17	**20.5**	1.21	44	6.8	**2.07**
165	12–17	**20**	1.24	45	7	**2.07**
165	12–17	**19.5**	1.28	46	7.1	**2.07**
165	12–17	**19**	1.31	47	7.3	**2.07**
165	12–17	**18.5**	1.34	48	7.4	**2.07**
165	12–17	**18**	1.38	50	7.8	**2.07**
165	12–17	**17.5**	1.42	51	7.9	**2.07**
165	12–17	**17**	1.46	53	8.2	**2.07**
165	12–17	**16.5**	1.51	54	8.4	**2.07**
165	12–17	**16**	1.55	56	8.7	**2.07**
165	12–17	**15.5**	1.6	58	9	**2.07**
165	12–17	**15**	1.66	60	9.3	**2.07**
165	12–17	**14.5**	1.72	62	9.6	**2.07**
165	12–17	**14**	1.78	64	9.9	**2.07**
165	12–17	**13.5**	1.84	66	10.2	**2.07**
165	12–17	**13**	1.91	69	10.7	**2.07**
165	12–17	**12.5**	1.99	72	11.2	**2.07**
165	12–17	**12**	2.07	75	11.6	**2.07**
166	12–17	**21**	1.18	42	6.5	**2.06**
166	12–17	**20.5**	1.21	43	6.7	**2.06**

A/L	Sizes	Body	1 sq.pi.	1 sq.in.	1 sq.cm.	Ch./pi.
166	12–17	**20**	1.24	45	7	**2.06**
166	12–17	**19.5**	1.27	46	7.1	**2.06**
166	12–17	**19**	1.3	47	7.3	**2.06**
166	12–17	**18.5**	1.34	48	7.4	**2.06**
166	12–17	**18**	1.37	49	7.6	**2.06**
166	12–17	**17.5**	1.41	51	7.9	**2.06**
166	12–17	**17**	1.45	52	8.1	**2.06**
166	12–17	**16.5**	1.5	54	8.4	**2.06**
166	12–17	**16**	1.55	56	8.7	**2.06**
166	12–17	**15.5**	1.6	57	8.8	**2.06**
166	12–17	**15**	1.65	59	9.1	**2.06**
166	12–17	**14.5**	1.71	61	9.5	**2.06**
166	12–17	**14**	1.77	64	9.9	**2.06**
166	12–17	**13.5**	1.83	66	10.2	**2.06**
166	12–17	**13**	1.9	68	10.5	**2.06**
166	12–17	**12.5**	1.98	71	11	**2.06**
166	12–17	**12**	2.06	74	11.5	**2.06**
167	12–17	**21**	1.17	42	6.5	**2.05**
167	12–17	**20.5**	1.2	43	6.7	**2.05**
167	12–17	**20**	1.23	44	6.8	**2.05**
167	12–17	**19.5**	1.26	45	7	**2.05**
167	12–17	**19**	1.29	47	7.3	**2.05**
167	12–17	**18.5**	1.33	48	7.4	**2.05**
167	12–17	**18**	1.37	49	7.6	**2.05**
167	12–17	**17.5**	1.4	51	7.9	**2.05**
167	12–17	**17**	1.45	52	8.1	**2.05**
167	12–17	**16.5**	1.49	54	8.4	**2.05**
167	12–17	**16**	1.54	55	8.5	**2.05**
167	12–17	**15.5**	1.59	57	8.8	**2.05**
167	12–17	**15**	1.64	59	9.1	**2.05**
167	12–17	**14.5**	1.69	61	9.5	**2.05**
167	12–17	**14**	1.76	63	9.8	**2.05**
167	12–17	**13.5**	1.82	66	10.2	**2.05**
167	12–17	**13**	1.89	68	10.5	**2.05**
167	12–17	**12.5**	1.97	71	11	**2.05**
167	12–17	**12**	2.05	74	11.5	**2.05**
168	12–17	**21**	1.16	42	6.5	**2.04**
168	12–17	**20.5**	1.19	43	6.7	**2.04**
168	12–17	**20**	1.22	44	6.8	**2.04**
168	12–17	**19.5**	1.25	45	7	**2.04**
168	12–17	**19**	1.29	46	7.1	**2.04**
168	12–17	**18.5**	1.32	48	7.4	**2.04**
168	12–17	**18**	1.36	49	7.6	**2.04**
168	12–17	**17.5**	1.4	50	7.8	**2.04**

A/L	Sizes	Body	1 sq.pi.	1 sq.in.	1 sq.cm.	Ch./pi.
168	12–17	17	1.44	52	8.1	2.04
168	12–17	16.5	1.48	53	8.2	2.04
168	12–17	16	1.53	55	8.5	2.04
168	12–17	15.5	1.58	57	8.8	2.04
168	12–17	15	1.63	59	9.1	2.04
168	12–17	14.5	1.68	61	9.5	2.04
168	12–17	14	1.74	63	9.8	2.04
168	12–17	13.5	1.81	65	10.1	2.04
168	12–17	13	1.88	68	10.5	2.04
168	12–17	12.5	1.95	70	10.9	2.04
168	12–17	12	2.04	73	11.3	2.04
169	12–17	21	1.16	42	6.5	2.02
169	12–17	20.5	1.18	43	6.7	2.02
169	12–17	20	1.21	44	6.8	2.02
169	12–17	19.5	1.25	45	7	2.02
169	12–17	19	1.28	46	7.1	2.02
169	12–17	18.5	1.31	47	7.3	2.02
169	12–17	18	1.35	49	7.6	2.02
169	12–17	17.5	1.39	50	7.8	2.02
169	12–17	17	1.43	51	7.9	2.02
169	12–17	16.5	1.47	53	8.2	2.02
169	12–17	16	1.52	55	8.5	2.02
169	12–17	15.5	1.57	56	8.7	2.02
169	12–17	15	1.62	58	9	2.02
169	12–17	14.5	1.67	60	9.3	2.02
169	12–17	14	1.73	62	9.6	2.02
169	12–17	13.5	1.8	65	10.1	2.02
169	12–17	13	1.87	67	10.4	2.02
169	12–17	12.5	1.94	70	10.9	2.02
169	12–17	12	2.02	73	11.3	2.02
170	12–17	21	1.15	41	6.4	2.01
170	12–17	20.5	1.18	42	6.5	2.01
170	12–17	20	1.21	43	6.7	2.01
170	12–17	19.5	1.24	45	7	2.01
170	12–17	19	1.27	46	7.1	2.01
170	12–17	18.5	1.3	47	7.3	2.01
170	12–17	18	1.34	48	7.4	2.01
170	12–17	17.5	1.38	50	7.8	2.01
170	12–17	17	1.42	51	7.9	2.01
170	12–17	16.5	1.46	53	8.2	2.01
170	12–17	16	1.51	54	8.4	2.01
170	12–17	15.5	1.56	56	8.7	2.01
170	12–17	15	1.61	58	9	2.01
170	12–17	14.5	1.66	60	9.3	2.01

A/L	Sizes	Body	1 sq.pi.	1 sq.in.	1 sq.cm.	Ch./pi.
170	12–17	**14**	1.72	62	9.6	**2.01**
170	12–17	**13.5**	1.79	64	9.9	**2.01**
170	12–17	**13**	1.86	67	10.4	**2.01**
170	12–17	**12.5**	1.93	70	10.9	**2.01**
170	12–17	**12**	2.01	72	11.2	**2.01**

TABLE 2 CHARACTERS PER PICA FOR DISPLAY SIZES OF INITIAL CAP AND LOWER CASE (ABOUT 13 TO 72 POINT)

(Note: Alphabet lengths given in picas)

A/L in picas	Chars. per pica	A/L in picas	Chars. per pica	A/L in picas	Chars. per pica
14	2.08	26	1.12	50	.58
14.25	2.05	26.5	1.10	51	.57
14.5	2.01	27	1.08	52	.56
14.75	1.98	27.5	1.06	53	.55
15	1.94	28	1.04	54	.54
15.25	1.91	28.5	1.02	55	.53
15.5	1.88	29	1.01	56	.52
15.75	1.85	29.5	.99	57	.51
16	1.82	30	.97	58	.50
16.25	1.79	30.5	.96	59	.49
16.5	1.77	31	.94	60	.49
16.75	1.74	31.5	.93	61	.48
17	1.72	32	.91	62	.47
17.25	1.69	32.5	.90	63	.46
17.5	1.67	33	.88	64	.46
17.75	1.64	33.5	.87	65	.45
18	1.62	34	.86	66	.44
18.25	1.60	34.5	.85	67	.44
18.5	1.58	35	.83	68	.43
18.75	1.56	35.5	.82	69	.42
19	1.54	36	.81	70	.42
19.25	1.52	36.5	.80	71	.41
19.5	1.50	37	.79	72	.41
19.75	1.48	37.5	.78	73	.40
20	1.46	38	.77	74	.39
20.25	1.44	38.5	.79	75	.39
20.5	1.42	39	.75	76	.38
20.75	1.41	39.5	.74	77	.38
21	1.39	40	.73	78	.37
21.25	1.37	40.5	.72	79	.37
21.5	1.36	41	.71	80	.36
21.75	1.34	41.5	.70	81	.36
22	1.33	42	.69	82	.36
22.25	1.31	42.5	.69	83	.35
22.5	1.30	43	.68	84	.35
22.75	1.28	43.5	.67	85	.34
23	1.27	44	.66	86	.34
23.25	1.25	44.5	.66	87	.34
23.5	1.24	45	.65	88	.33
23.75	1.23	45.5	.64	89	.33
24	1.22	46	.63	90	.32
24.25	1.20	41.5	.63	91	.32
24.5	1.19	47	.62	92	.32
24.75	1.18	47.5	.61	93	.31
25	1.17	48	.61	94	.31
25.25	1.16	48.5	.60	95	.31
25.5	1.14	49	.60	96	.30
25.75	1.13	49.5	.59	97	.30

TABLE 3 CHARACTERS PER PICA FOR CAPITAL LETTERS ABOUT 6 TO 60 POINT. NO LETTERSPACING. MACHINE SET.

(Note: Alphabet lengths given in picas)

A/L in picas	Chars. per pica	A/L in picas	Chars. per pica	A/L in picas	Chars. per pica
6	4.93	18	1.64	42	.70
6.25	4.73	18.5	1.60	43	.69
6.5	4.55	19	1.56	44	.67
6.75	4.38	19.5	1.52	45	.66
7	4.23	20	1.48	46	.64
7.25	4.08	20.5	1.44	47	.63
7.5	3.94	21	1.41	48	.62
7.75	3.82	21.5	1.38	49	.60
8	3.70	22	1.34	50	.59
8.25	3.59	22.5	1.31	51	.58
8.5	3.48	23	1.29	52	.57
8.75	3.38	23.5	1.26	53	.56
9	3.29	24	1.23	54	.55
9.25	3.20	24.5	1.21	55	.54
9.5	3.11	25	1.18	56	.53
9.75	3.03	25.5	1.16	57	.52
10	2.96	26	1.14	58	.51
10.25	2.89	26.5	1.12	59	.50
10.5	2.82	27	1.10	60	.49
10.75	2.75	27.5	1.08	61	.48
11	2.69	28	1.06	62	.48
11.25	2.63	28.5	1.04	63	.47
11.5	2.57	29	1.02	64	.46
11.75	2.52	29.5	1.00	65	.46
12	2.47	30	.99	66	.45
12.25	2.41	30.5	.97	67	.44
12.5	2.37	31	.95	68	.44
12.75	2.32	31.5	.94	69	.43
13	2.28	32	.92	70	.42
13.25	2.23	32.5	.91	71	.42
13.5	2.19	33	.90	72	.41
13.75	2.15	33.5	.88	73	.41
14	2.11	34	.87	74	.40
14.25	2.08	34.5	.86	75	.39
14.5	2.04	35	.85	76	.39
14.75	2.01	35.5	.83	77	.38
15	1.97	36	.82	78	.38
15.25	1.94	36.5	.81	79	.37
15.5	1.91	37	.80	80	.37
15.75	1.88	37.5	.79	81	.37
16	1.85	38	.78	82	.36
16.25	1.82	38.5	.77	83	.36
16.5	1.79	39	.76	84	.35
16.75	1.77	39.5	.75	85	.35
17	1.74	40	.74	86	.34
17.25	1.71	40.5	.73	87	.34
17.5	1.69	41	.72	88	.34
17.75	1.67	41.5	.71	89	.33

TABLE 4 CHARACTERS PER LINE BY ALPHABET LENGTH
FOR TEXT SIZES SET FROM 10 TO 30 PICAS

A/L	10	10.5	11	11.5	12	12.5	13	13.5	14	14.5	15	15.5	16	16.5	17	17.5	18	18.5	19	19.5	20
90	38	40	42	44	46	48	49	51	53	55	57	59	61	63	65	67	68	70	72	74	76
91	38	39	41	43	45	47	49	51	53	54	56	58	60	62	64	66	68	70	71	73	75
92	37	39	41	43	45	46	48	50	52	54	56	58	59	61	63	65	67	69	71	72	74
93	37	39	40	42	44	46	48	50	51	53	55	57	59	61	63	64	66	68	70	72	74
94	36	38	40	42	44	45	47	49	51	53	55	56	58	60	62	64	65	67	69	71	73
95	36	38	40	41	43	45	47	49	50	52	54	56	58	59	61	63	65	67	68	70	72
96	36	37	39	41	43	45	46	48	50	52	53	55	57	59	61	62	64	66	68	69	71
97	35	37	39	41	42	44	46	48	49	51	53	55	56	58	60	62	63	65	67	69	71
98	35	37	38	40	42	44	45	47	49	51	52	54	56	58	59	61	63	65	66	68	70
99	35	36	38	40	41	43	45	47	48	50	52	54	55	57	59	60	62	64	66	67	69
100	34	36	38	39	41	43	44	46	48	50	51	53	55	56	58	60	62	63	65	67	68
101	34	36	37	39	41	42	44	46	47	49	51	52	54	56	58	59	61	63	64	66	68
102	34	35	37	39	40	42	44	45	47	49	50	52	54	55	57	59	60	62	64	65	67
103	33	35	37	38	40	42	43	45	46	48	50	51	53	55	56	58	60	61	63	65	66
104	33	35	36	38	39	41	43	44	46	48	49	51	53	54	56	58	59	61	62	64	66
105	33	34	36	37	39	41	42	44	46	47	49	50	52	54	55	57	59	60	62	64	65
106	32	34	35	37	39	40	42	44	45	47	48	50	52	53	55	56	58	60	61	63	65
107	32	34	35	37	38	40	42	43	45	46	48	50	51	53	54	56	58	59	61	62	64
108	32	33	35	36	38	40	41	43	44	46	47	49	51	52	54	55	57	59	60	62	63
109	31	33	35	36	38	39	41	42	44	45	47	49	50	52	53	55	56	58	60	61	63
110	31	33	34	36	37	39	40	42	44	45	47	48	50	51	53	54	56	58	59	61	62
111	31	32	34	35	37	39	40	42	43	45	46	48	49	51	52	54	55	57	59	60	62
112	31	32	34	35	37	38	40	41	43	44	46	47	49	50	52	53	55	56	58	60	61
113	30	32	33	35	36	38	39	41	42	44	45	47	48	50	51	53	54	56	58	59	61
114	30	32	33	35	36	38	39	41	42	44	45	47	48	50	51	53	54	56	57	59	60
115	30	31	33	34	36	37	39	40	42	43	45	46	48	49	51	52	54	55	57	58	59
116	29	31	32	34	35	37	38	40	41	43	44	46	47	49	50	52	53	55	56	57	59
117	29	31	32	34	35	37	38	39	41	42	44	45	47	48	50	51	53	54	56	57	58
118	29	30	32	33	35	36	38	39	41	42	43	45	46	48	49	51	52	54	55	57	58
119	29	30	32	33	34	36	37	39	40	42	43	45	46	47	49	50	52	53	55	56	57
120	29	30	31	33	34	36	37	38	40	41	43	44	46	47	48	50	51	53	54	56	57
121	28	30	31	33	34	35	37	38	40	41	42	44	45	47	48	49	51	52	54	55	57
122	28	29	31	32	34	35	36	38	39	41	42	43	45	46	48	49	50	52	53	55	56
123	28	29	31	32	33	35	36	38	39	40	42	43	44	46	47	49	50	51	53	54	56
124	28	29	30	32	33	34	36	37	39	40	41	43	44	46	47	48	50	51	52	54	55
125	27	29	30	31	33	34	36	37	38	40	41	42	44	45	47	48	49	51	52	53	55
126	27	28	30	31	33	34	35	37	38	39	41	42	43	45	46	47	49	50	52	53	54
127	27	28	30	31	32	34	35	36	38	39	40	42	43	44	46	47	48	50	51	53	54
128	27	28	29	31	32	33	35	36	37	39	40	41	43	44	45	47	48	49	51	52	53
129	27	28	29	30	32	33	34	36	37	38	40	41	42	44	45	46	48	49	50	52	53
130	26	28	29	30	32	33	34	36	37	38	39	41	42	43	45	46	47	49	50	51	53

ALPHABET LENGTH IN POINTS

WIDTH OF LINE IN PICAS

A/L	20.5	21	21.5	22	22.5	23	23.5	24	24.5	25	25.5	26	26.5	27	27.5	28	28.5	29	29.5	30	30.5
90	78	80	82	84	86	87	89	91	93	95	97	99	101	103	105	106	108	110	112	114	116
91	77	79	81	83	85	86	88	90	92	94	96	98	100	101	103	105	107	109	111	113	115
92	76	78	80	82	84	85	87	89	91	93	95	97	99	100	102	104	106	108	110	112	113
93	75	77	79	81	83	85	86	88	90	92	94	96	97	99	101	103	105	107	108	110	112
94	75	76	78	80	82	84	85	87	89	91	93	95	96	98	100	102	104	106	107	109	111
95	74	76	77	79	81	83	85	86	88	90	92	94	95	97	99	101	103	104	106	108	110
96	73	75	77	78	80	82	84	86	87	89	91	93	94	96	98	100	102	103	105	107	109
97	72	74	76	78	79	81	83	85	86	88	90	92	93	95	97	99	100	102	104	106	108
98	72	73	75	77	79	80	82	84	85	87	89	91	92	94	96	98	99	101	103	105	106
99	71	73	74	76	78	79	81	83	85	86	88	90	92	93	95	97	98	100	102	104	105
100	70	72	74	75	77	79	80	82	84	86	87	89	91	92	94	96	97	99	101	103	104
101	69	71	73	74	76	78	80	81	83	85	86	88	90	91	93	95	97	98	100	102	103
102	69	70	72	74	75	77	79	80	82	84	85	87	89	91	92	94	96	97	99	101	102
103	68	70	71	73	75	76	78	80	81	83	85	86	88	90	91	93	95	96	98	100	101
104	67	69	71	72	74	76	77	79	81	82	84	85	87	89	90	92	94	95	97	99	100
105	67	68	70	72	73	75	77	78	80	81	83	85	86	88	90	91	93	94	96	98	99
106	66	68	69	71	73	74	76	77	79	81	82	84	85	87	89	90	92	94	95	97	98
107	66	67	69	70	72	74	75	77	78	80	82	83	85	86	88	89	90	93	94	96	97
108	65	66	68	70	71	73	74	76	78	79	81	82	84	85	87	89	90	92	93	95	97
109	64	66	67	69	71	72	74	75	77	78	80	82	83	85	86	88	89	91	93	94	96
110	64	65	67	68	70	72	73	75	76	78	79	81	82	84	85	87	89	90	92	93	95
111	63	65	66	68	69	71	72	74	75	77	79	80	82	83	85	86	88	89	91	92	94
112	63	64	66	67	69	70	72	73	75	76	78	79	81	82	84	85	87	89	90	92	93
113	62	64	65	67	68	70	71	73	74	76	77	79	80	82	83	85	86	88	89	91	92
114	62	63	65	66	68	69	71	72	74	75	77	78	80	81	83	84	86	87	89	90	92
115	61	62	64	65	67	68	70	71	73	74	76	77	79	80	82	83	85	86	88	89	91
116	60	62	63	65	66	68	69	71	72	74	75	77	78	80	81	83	84	85	87	88	90
117	60	61	63	64	66	67	69	70	72	73	75	76	77	79	80	82	83	85	86	88	89
118	59	61	62	64	65	67	68	70	71	72	74	75	77	78	80	81	83	84	85	87	88
119	59	60	62	63	65	66	68	69	70	72	73	75	76	78	79	80	82	83	85	86	88
120	58	60	61	63	64	66	67	68	70	71	73	74	76	77	78	80	81	83	84	86	87
121	58	59	61	62	64	65	66	68	69	71	72	73	75	76	78	79	81	82	83	85	86
122	57	59	60	62	63	64	66	67	69	70	71	73	74	76	77	78	80	81	83	84	85
123	57	58	60	61	63	64	65	67	68	70	71	72	74	75	76	78	79	81	82	83	85
124	57	58	59	61	62	63	65	66	68	69	70	72	73	74	76	77	79	80	81	83	84
125	56	57	59	60	62	63	64	66	67	68	70	71	73	74	75	77	78	79	81	82	83
126	56	57	58	60	61	62	64	65	66	68	69	71	72	73	75	76	77	79	80	81	83
127	55	57	58	59	61	62	63	65	66	67	69	70	71	73	74	75	77	78	79	81	82
128	55	56	57	59	60	61	63	64	65	67	68	69	71	72	73	75	76	77	79	80	81
129	54	56	57	58	60	61	62	64	65	66	68	69	70	72	73	74	76	77	78	80	81
130	54	55	57	58	59	61	62	63	64	66	67	68	70	71	72	74	75	76	78	79	80

WIDTH OF LINE IN PICAS

TABLE 5 DEPTH OF TYPE AREA (IN PICAS) FOR A GIVEN NUMBER OF LINES

Lines	5 pt	5½ pt	6 pt	6½ pt	7 pt	7½ pt	8 pt	8½ pt	9 pt	9½ pt	10 pt	10½ pt	11 pt	11½ pt
1	.43	.47	.51	.55	.59	.64	.68	.72	.76	.80	.84	.89	.93	.97
2	.84	.93	1.01	1.09	1.18	1.26	1.34	1.43	1.51	1.59	1.68	1.76	1.84	1.93
3	1.26	1.39	1.51	1.64	1.76	1.89	2.01	2.14	2.26	2.39	2.51	2.64	2.76	2.89
4	1.68	1.84	2.01	2.18	2.34	2.51	2.68	2.84	3.01	3.18	3.34	3.51	3.68	3.84
5	2.09	2.30	2.51	2.72	2.93	3.14	3.34	3.55	3.76	3.97	4.18	4.39	4.59	4.80
6	2.51	2.76	3.01	3.26	3.51	3.76	4.01	4.26	4.51	4.76	5.01	5.26	5.51	5.76
7	2.93	3.22	3.51	3.80	4.09	4.39	4.68	4.97	5.26	5.55	5.84	6.14	6.43	6.72
8	3.34	3.68	4.01	4.34	4.68	5.01	5.34	5.68	6.01	6.34	6.68	7.01	7.34	7.68
9	3.76	4.14	4.51	4.89	5.26	5.64	6.01	6.39	6.76	7.14	7.51	7.89	8.26	8.64
10	4.18	4.59	5.01	5.43	5.84	6.26	6.68	7.09	7.51	7.93	8.34	8.76	9.18	9.59
11	4.59	5.05	5.51	5.97	6.43	6.89	7.34	7.80	8.26	8.72	9.18	9.64	10.09	10.55
12	5.01	5.51	6.01	6.51	7.01	7.51	8.01	8.51	9.01	9.51	10.01	10.51	11.01	11.51
13	5.43	5.97	6.51	7.05	7.59	8.14	8.68	9.22	9.76	10.30	10.84	11.39	11.93	12.47
14	5.84	6.43	7.01	7.59	8.18	8.76	9.34	9.93	10.51	11.09	11.68	12.26	12.84	13.43
15	6.26	6.89	7.51	8.14	8.76	9.39	10.01	10.64	11.26	11.89	12.51	13.14	13.76	14.39
16	6.68	7.34	8.01	8.68	9.34	10.01	10.68	11.34	12.01	12.68	13.34	14.01	14.68	15.34
17	7.09	7.80	8.51	9.22	9.93	10.64	11.34	12.05	12.76	13.47	14.18	14.89	15.59	16.30
18	7.51	8.26	9.01	9.76	10.51	11.26	12.01	12.76	13.51	14.26	15.01	15.76	16.51	17.26
19	7.93	8.72	9.51	10.30	11.09	11.89	12.68	13.47	14.26	15.05	15.84	16.64	17.43	18.22
20	8.34	9.18	10.01	10.84	11.68	12.51	13.34	14.18	15.01	15.84	16.68	17.51	18.34	19.18
21	8.76	9.64	10.51	11.39	12.26	13.14	14.01	14.89	15.76	16.64	17.51	18.39	19.26	20.14
22	9.18	10.09	11.01	11.93	12.84	13.76	14.68	15.59	16.51	17.43	18.34	19.26	20.18	21.09
23	9.59	10.55	11.51	12.47	13.43	14.39	15.34	16.30	17.26	18.22	19.18	20.14	21.09	22.05
24	10.01	11.01	12.01	13.01	14.01	15.01	16.01	17.01	18.01	19.01	20.01	21.01	22.01	23.01
25	10.43	11.47	12.51	13.55	14.59	15.64	16.68	17.72	18.76	19.80	20.84	21.89	22.93	23.97
26	10.84	11.93	13.01	14.09	15.18	16.26	17.34	18.43	19.51	20.59	21.68	22.76	23.84	24.93
27	11.26	12.39	13.51	14.64	15.76	16.89	18.01	19.14	20.26	21.39	22.51	23.64	24.76	25.89
28	11.68	12.84	14.01	15.18	16.34	17.51	18.68	19.84	21.01	22.18	23.34	24.51	25.68	26.84
29	12.09	13.30	14.51	15.72	16.93	18.14	19.34	20.55	21.76	22.97	24.18	25.39	26.59	27.80
30	12.51	13.76	15.01	16.26	17.51	18.76	20.01	21.26	22.51	23.76	25.01	26.26	27.51	28.76
31	12.93	14.22	15.51	16.80	18.09	19.39	20.68	21.97	23.26	24.55	25.84	27.14	28.43	29.72
32	13.34	14.68	16.01	17.34	18.68	20.01	21.34	22.68	24.01	25.34	26.68	28.01	29.34	30.68
33	13.76	15.14	16.51	17.89	19.26	20.64	22.01	23.39	24.76	26.14	27.51	28.89	30.26	31.64
34	14.18	15.59	17.01	18.43	19.84	21.26	22.68	24.09	25.51	26.93	28.34	29.76	31.18	32.59
35	14.59	16.05	17.51	18.97	20.43	21.89	23.34	24.80	26.26	27.72	29.18	30.64	32.09	33.55
36	15.01	16.51	18.01	19.51	21.01	22.51	24.01	25.51	27.01	28.51	30.01	31.51	33.01	34.51
37	15.43	16.97	18.51	20.05	21.59	23.14	24.68	26.22	27.76	29.30	30.84	32.39	33.93	35.47
38	15.84	17.43	19.01	20.59	22.18	23.76	25.34	26.93	28.51	30.09	31.68	33.26	34.84	36.43
39	16.26	17.89	19.51	21.14	22.76	24.39	26.01	27.64	29.26	30.89	32.51	34.14	35.76	37.39
40	16.68	18.34	20.01	21.68	23.34	25.01	26.68	28.34	30.01	31.68	33.34	35.01	36.68	38.34
41	17.09	18.80	20.51	22.22	23.93	25.64	27.34	29.05	30.76	32.47	34.18	35.89	37.59	39.30
42	17.51	19.26	21.01	22.76	24.51	26.26	28.01	29.76	31.51	33.26	35.01	36.76	38.51	40.26
43	17.93	19.72	21.51	23.30	25.09	26.89	28.68	30.47	32.26	34.05	35.84	37.64	39.43	41.22
44	18.34	20.18	22.01	23.84	25.68	27.51	29.34	31.18	33.01	34.84	36.68	38.51	40.34	42.18
45	18.76	20.64	22.51	24.39	26.26	28.14	30.01	31.89	33.76	35.64	37.51	39.39	41.26	43.14

Lines	5 pt	5½ pt	6 pt	6½ pt	7 pt	7½ pt	8 pt	8½ pt	9 pt	9½ pt	10 pt	10½ pt	11 pt	11½ pt
46	19.18	21.09	23.01	24.93	26.84	28.76	30.68	32.59	34.51	36.43	38.34	40.26	42.18	44.09
47	19.59	21.55	23.51	25.47	27.43	29.39	31.34	33.30	35.26	37.22	39.18	41.14	43.09	45.05
48	20.01	22.01	24.01	26.01	28.01	30.01	32.01	34.01	36.01	38.01	40.01	42.01	44.01	46.01
49	20.43	22.47	24.51	26.55	28.59	30.64	32.68	34.72	36.76	38.80	40.84	42.89	44.93	46.97
50	20.84	22.93	25.01	27.09	29.18	31.26	33.34	35.43	37.51	39.59	41.68	43.76	45.84	47.93
51	21.26	23.39	25.51	27.64	29.76	31.89	34.01	36.14	38.26	40.39	42.51	44.64	46.76	48.89
52	21.68	23.84	26.01	28.18	30.34	32.51	34.68	36.84	39.01	41.18	43.34	45.51	47.68	49.84
53	22.09	24.30	26.51	28.72	30.93	33.14	35.34	37.55	39.76	41.97	44.18	46.39	48.59	50.80
54	22.51	24.76	27.01	29.26	31.51	33.76	36.01	38.26	40.51	42.76	45.01	47.26	49.51	51.76
55	22.93	25.22	27.51	29.80	32.09	34.39	36.68	38.97	41.26	43.55	45.84	48.14	50.43	52.72
56	23.34	25.68	28.01	30.34	32.68	35.01	37.34	39.68	42.01	44.34	46.68	49.01	51.34	53.68
57	23.76	26.14	28.51	30.89	33.26	35.64	38.01	40.39	42.76	45.14	47.51	49.89	52.26	54.64
58	24.18	26.59	29.01	31.43	33.84	36.26	38.68	41.09	43.51	45.93	48.34	50.76	53.18	55.59
59	24.59	27.05	29.51	31.97	34.43	36.89	39.34	41.80	44.26	46.72	49.18	51.64	54.09	56.55
60	25.01	27.51	30.01	32.51	35.01	37.51	40.01	42.51	45.01	47.51	50.01	52.51	55.01	57.51
61	25.43	27.97	30.51	33.05	35.59	38.14	40.68	43.22	45.76	48.30	50.84	53.39	55.93	58.47
62	25.84	28.43	31.01	33.59	36.18	38.76	41.34	43.93	46.51	49.09	51.68	54.26	56.84	59.43
63	26.26	28.89	31.51	34.14	36.76	39.39	42.01	44.64	47.26	49.89	52.51	55.14	57.76	60.39
64	26.68	29.34	32.01	34.68	37.34	40.01	42.68	45.34	48.01	50.68	53.34	56.01	58.68	
65	27.09	29.80	32.51	35.22	37.93	40.64	43.34	46.05	48.76	51.47	54.18	56.89	59.59	
66	27.51	30.26	33.01	35.76	38.51	41.26	44.01	46.76	49.51	52.26	55.01	57.76	60.51	
67	27.93	30.72	33.51	36.30	39.09	41.89	44.68	47.47	50.26	53.05	55.84	58.64		
68	28.34	31.18	34.01	36.84	39.68	42.51	45.34	48.18	51.01	53.84	56.68	59.51		
69	28.76	31.64	34.51	37.39	40.26	43.14	46.01	48.89	51.76	54.64	57.51	60.39		
70	29.18	32.09	35.01	37.93	40.84	43.76	46.68	49.59	52.51	55.43	58.34			
71	29.59	32.55	35.51	38.47	41.43	44.39	47.34	50.30	53.26	56.22	59.18			
72	30.01	33.01	36.01	39.01	42.01	45.01	48.01	51.01	54.01	57.01	60.01			
73	30.43	33.47	36.51	39.55	42.59	45.64	48.68	51.72	54.76	57.80				
74	30.84	33.93	37.01	40.09	43.18	46.26	49.34	52.43	55.51	58.59				
75	31.26	34.39	37.51	40.64	43.76	46.89	50.01	53.14	56.26	59.39				
76	31.68	34.84	38.01	41.18	44.34	47.51	50.68	53.84	57.01	60.18				
77	32.09	35.30	38.51	41.72	44.93	48.14	51.34	54.55	57.76					
78	32.51	35.76	39.01	42.26	45.51	48.76	52.01	55.26	58.51					
79	32.93	36.22	39.51	42.80	46.09	49.39	52.68	55.97	59.26					
80	33.34	36.68	40.01	43.34	46.68	50.01	53.34	56.68	60.01					
81	33.76	37.14	40.51	43.89	47.26	50.64	54.01	57.39						
82	34.18	37.59	41.01	44.43	47.84	51.26	54.68	58.09						
83	34.59	38.05	41.51	44.97	48.43	51.89	55.34	58.80						
84	35.01	38.51	42.01	45.51	49.01	52.51	56.01	59.51						
85	35.43	38.97	42.51	46.05	49.59	53.14	56.68	60.22						
86	35.84	39.43	43.01	46.59	50.18	53.76	57.34							
87	36.26	39.89	43.51	47.14	50.76	54.39	58.01							
88	36.68	40.34	44.01	47.68	51.34	55.01	58.68							
89	37.09	40.80	44.51	48.22	51.93	55.64	59.34							
90	37.51	41.26	45.01	48.76	52.51	56.26	60.01							

(Continued on next page)

55

TABLE 5 (CONT.) DEPTH OF TYPE AREA (IN PICAS) FOR A GIVEN NUMBER OF LINES

Lines	13 pt	14 pt	15 pt	16 pt	17 pt	18 pt	19 pt	20 pt	21 pt	22 pt	23 pt
1	1.09	1.18	1.26	1.34	1.43	1.51	1.59	1.68	1.76	1.84	1.93
2	2.18	2.34	2.51	2.68	2.84	3.01	3.18	3.34	3.51	3.68	3.84
3	3.26	3.51	3.76	4.01	4.26	4.51	4.76	5.01	5.26	5.51	5.76
4	4.34	4.68	5.01	5.34	5.68	6.01	6.34	6.68	7.01	7.34	7.68
5	5.43	5.84	6.26	6.68	7.09	7.51	7.93	8.34	8.76	9.18	9.59
6	6.51	7.01	7.51	8.01	8.51	9.01	9.51	10.01	10.51	11.01	11.51
7	7.59	8.18	8.76	9.34	9.93	10.51	11.09	11.68	12.26	12.84	13.43
8	8.68	9.34	10.01	10.68	11.34	12.01	12.68	13.34	14.01	14.68	15.34
9	9.76	10.51	11.26	12.01	12.76	13.51	14.26	15.01	15.76	16.51	17.26
10	10.84	11.68	12.51	13.34	14.18	15.01	15.84	16.68	17.51	18.34	19.18
11	11.93	12.84	13.76	14.68	15.59	16.51	17.43	18.34	19.26	20.18	21.09
12	13.01	14.01	15.01	16.01	17.01	18.01	19.01	20.01	21.01	22.01	23.01
13	14.09	15.18	16.26	17.34	18.43	19.51	20.59	21.68	22.76	23.84	24.93
14	15.18	16.34	17.51	18.68	19.84	21.01	22.18	23.34	24.51	25.68	26.84
15	16.26	17.51	18.76	20.01	21.26	22.51	23.76	25.01	26.26	27.51	28.76
16	17.34	18.68	20.01	21.34	22.68	24.01	25.34	26.68	28.01	29.34	30.68
17	18.43	19.84	21.26	22.68	24.09	25.51	26.93	28.34	29.76	31.18	32.59
18	19.51	21.01	22.51	24.01	25.51	27.01	28.51	30.01	31.51	33.01	34.51
19	20.59	22.18	23.76	25.34	26.93	28.51	30.09	31.68	33.26	34.84	36.43
20	21.68	23.34	25.01	26.68	28.34	30.01	31.68	33.34	35.01	36.68	38.34
21	22.76	24.51	26.26	28.01	29.76	31.51	33.26	35.01	36.76	38.51	40.26
22	23.84	25.68	27.51	29.34	31.18	33.01	34.84	36.68	38.51	40.34	42.18
23	24.93	26.84	28.76	30.68	32.59	34.51	36.43	38.34	40.26	42.18	44.09
24	26.01	28.01	30.01	32.01	34.01	36.01	38.01	40.01	42.01	44.01	46.01
25	27.09	29.18	31.26	33.34	35.43	37.51	39.59	41.68	43.76	45.84	47.98
26	28.18	30.34	32.51	34.68	36.84	39.01	41.18	43.34	45.51	47.68	49.84
27	29.26	31.51	33.76	36.01	38.26	40.51	42.76	45.01	47.26	49.51	51.76
28	30.34	32.68	35.01	37.34	39.68	42.01	44.34	46.68	49.01	51.34	53.68
29	31.43	33.84	36.26	38.68	41.09	43.51	45.93	48.34	50.76	53.18	55.59
30	32.51	35.01	37.51	40.01	42.51	45.01	47.51	50.01	52.51	55.01	57.51
31	33.59	36.18	38.76	41.34	43.93	46.51	49.09	51.68	54.26	56.84	59.43
32	34.68	37.34	40.01	42.68	45.34	48.01	50.68	53.34	56.01	58.68	61.34
33	35.76	38.51	41.26	44.01	46.76	49.51	52.26	55.01	57.76	60.51	
34	36.84	39.68	42.51	45.34	48.18	51.01	53.84	56.68	59.51		
35	37.93	40.84	43.76	46.68	49.59	52.51	55.43	58.34	61.26		
36	39.01	42.01	45.01	48.01	51.01	54.01	57.01	60.01			
37	40.09	43.18	46.26	49.34	52.43	55.51	58.59				
38	41.18	44.34	47.51	50.68	53.84	57.01	60.18				
39	42.26	45.51	48.76	52.01	55.26	58.51					
40	43.34	46.68	50.01	53.34	56.68	60.01					
41	44.43	47.84	51.26	54.68	58.09						
42	45.51	49.01	52.51	56.01	59.51						
43	46.59	50.18	53.76	57.34	60.93						
44	47.68	51.34	55.01	58.68							
45	48.76	52.51	56.26	60.01							
46	49.84	53.68	57.51								
47	50.93	54.84	58.76								
48	52.01	56.01	60.01								
49	53.09	57.18									
50	54.18	58.34									
51	55.26	59.51									
52	56.34	60.68									
53	57.43										
54	58.51										
55	59.59										
56	60.68										

APPENDIX A
Castoff-related programs for programmable pocket calculators

The general availability of rather simple and inexpensive* programmable pocket calculators (and people interested in working with them) makes it worthwhile to include in this book some reference programs for various aspects of castoff and copy fitting. The programs are quite simple and are written in a generalized descriptive-algebraic notation that will not be outdated by new calculators. Using any programmable calculator, the programs can be adapted with little effort to the slightly differing notations and capabilities available. They are intended to be suggestive as to method. Some are perhaps most useful to write tables.

Only the essentials are required by these programs: 10 storage registers (0–9) and about 100 (maximum) steps of program, usually a good deal less. No printer is needed and no separate storage of programs, magnetic cards, or otherwise, although if available these can naturally be used to advantage.

Some familiarity with the programmable calculator will be helpful, but although it may be useful for the designer, estimator, or production person to have such familiarity, it is not essential for most people. Useful work (such as reference tables) can often be done as a favor by a friend who is a calculator enthusiast but who may know nothing of castoff problems. The following should be a sufficient guide.

Terms used in the programs
Terminology has been kept simple, and no special notations have been used.

Register: A storage location that can store a numerical value (Reg. 0 to Reg. 9).
To store: To press a key that stores in a named register the value currently shown in the visual display.
To recall: To press a key that recalls to the visual display whatever value is currently stored in the named register.

    EXAMPLE: 6/Recall-5 = Store-1
    TRANSLATION: 6 is to be divided by the value currently stored in Reg. 5, and the result (equals) is then to be stored in Reg. 1.

Run/start (R/S): This key is sometimes called "run/stop." It stops, starts, or

---

*About $40. to $100. (1979). The Texas Instruments SR56 is typical.

restarts the program exactly *from the point it currently is*. It starts the program running, and restarts it every time after it stops to display an answer. Hence it is to be keyed by the user after each "STOP" indicated in the programs that follow.* It has not been thought necessary to indicate this every time.

Reset: This key indicates that the program is to start again at the beginning. The user keys it only to make sure that a program starts at the beginning (as indicated under "In use"). Most often it is part of the program, as will be noted.

Equals sign (=): This indicates that the program is to complete any operations that may be pending.

Parentheses are used as necessary to clarify algebraic expressions, and inner parentheses are evaluated by the program before the outer parentheses. Division is indicated by the slash: /.

Answers are delivered by the program at places indicated by the word STOP. The running of the program stops at that point and the user notes the result shown in the display. (It is understood that the program must be started again from that point, from the keyboard, by means of the R/S key.) A "PAUSE" has sometimes been used in place of STOP, because it is available on some machines. It displays an answer for about one-half second and continues automatically. If it is not available, the user may simply substitute a STOP.

The aim of these programs is to provide clear logic and to allow a good deal of human judgment and program flexibility in use.

Answers are provided by the calculator one by one, in the visual display, about as fast as they are requested from the keyboard. For this reason an orderly way of recording them is required (especially in the absence of an auxiliary printer) in order to know exactly which answer is being shown at any moment, and to record it properly for future reference. Therefore, several forms are provided, to be filled in as the answers are obtained. The reader may wish to draw up other similar forms. Note: If you *do not* record data in an orderly way, the use of programs can be confusing. Make at least a rough form to record your results.

---

*For the person *programming*, STOP means run/*stop*.

1. FOR DIRECT CASTOFF OF MANUSCRIPT. *To convert lines or pages of manuscript into type pages and type lines, cumulatively and flexibly either by counting pages of manuscript (in pages and tenths) or lines of manuscript.*

Successive values of pages or lines are entered by the user into the display. The program cumulatively totals the results in book pages. Also, full book pages, such as illustrations, etc., can be added directly to the cumulative book page total. See **In use** #11.

Register 1 = characters per line of manuscript
Register 2 = characters per line of type
Register 3 = lines per page of type
Register 4 = lines per page of manuscript (used if counting manuscript pages)
Register 5 = (used by program for cumulative pages)
Register 6 = (used by program for cumulative lines)

The Program

× Recall-4 (*NOTE: Omit this line unless counting by ms. pages*)
× Recall-1/Recall-2 = (*lines of type, cumulative*)
Add (*lines of type*) to value in Reg. 6
Divide (*lines of type*) by Recall-3 = (*pages required for these ms. lines*)
Add these (*pages*) to value in Reg. 5
Recall-6, PAUSE (*1/2-second display of cumulative lines total*)
Recall-5   Fix 1 decimal for display
STOP   (*shows cumulative pages and tenths of page*)
Program resets to the beginning.

At STOP, the user observes the result, notes it if necessary, enters a new value for lines or pages (whichever is being counted), and presses R/S for run/start. Program resets to the beginning, and processes the new segment of information.

In use

1. Decide whether you want to count the manuscript by lines or by pages, since the program will not mix these. The dirtier (and shorter) the manuscript, the more counting by lines is indicated.
2. Enter the program into the calculator memory, omitting the first line if manuscript is being counted by lines.
3. Store the proper values in Regs. 1,2,3 (and 4 if counting the manuscript by pages).
4. Start the program at the beginning by pressing Reset.
5. Enter the first value of pages, or lines, of manuscript.
6. Press R/S key.
7. Simply observe the answers that appear in the display: first the lines are shown for $\frac{1}{2}$ second, then it stops on book pages. These values *accumulate*, so they need be noted only at critical points in the manuscript.
8. Enter the next value for pages or lines of manuscript, and repeat steps 6 and 7.

Continue doing this as long as there is manuscript left to count. Results are cumulative.

9. The values in Regs. 1–4 can be changed at any time as required. Also, if you notice that a mistake has been made, it can be corrected by entering negative values of lines or pages to compensate. (Enter the value and then change its sign before pressing R/S.)

10. To start again, or begin a new problem, or go back to a certain point in the castoff, the accumulated pages in Reg. 5 and the lines in Reg. 6 must be reset to zero, or to the desired number. Then key Reset, enter a new value for manuscript lines or pages, and key R/S as before.

11. To enter final book pages directly into the cumulative page total (eg., for illustrations), add them directly into Reg. 5. For example: "2.3 sum 5" will add 2.3 pages to the book total.

2. SPECIAL PURPOSE CASTOFF TABLES. *For user-defined page and type specification ranges, this generates tables of lines per page, characters per page, factors for elite and pica typewriter conversions to type pages, words per page, and text pages per 100,000 characters of manuscript. (See the sample table below. The table in Appendix B has the same form.)*

CASTOFF RESULTS: FOR 6″ × 9″ TRIMMED SIZE (Per 100,000 Characters ms)

A. For typefaces with 2.50 to 2.59 characters per pica (e.g., 10 pt VIP Baskerville)

Type Body	Width (measure)	Depth	Lines/pg	Chars/pg	Elite* Factor	Pica* Factor	Words** book pg	Text pp/ 100M chars
11	26	43	47	3104	.65	.54	564	32.22
		44	48	3170	.64	.53	576	31.55
		45	49	3236	.63	.52	588	30.90
	27	43	47	3223	.63	.52	586	31.02
		44	48	3292	.62	.51	599	30.38
		45	49	3360	.60	.50	611	29.76
	28	43	47	3343	.61	.50	608	29.92
		44	48	3414	.59	.49	621	29.29
		45	49	3485	.58	.48	634	28.70
12	26	43	43	2840	.71	.59	516	35.21
		44	44	2906	.70	.58	528	34.41
		45	45	2972	.68	.56	540	33.65
	27	43	43	2949	.69	.57	536	33.91
		44	44	3018	.67	.56	549	33.14
		45	45	3086	.66	.54	561	32.40
	28	43	43	3058	.66	.55	556	32.70
		44	44	3129	.65	.54	569	31.96
		45	45	3200	.63	.52	582	31.25
13	26	43	39	2576	.79	.65	468	38.83
		44	40	2642	.77	.63	480	37.86
		45	41	2708	.75	.62	492	36.93
	27	43	39	2675	.76	.63	486	37.39
		44	40	2743	.74	.61	499	36.45
		45	41	2812	.72	.60	511	35.56
	28	43	39	2774	.73	.60	504	36.05
		44	40	2845	.71	.59	517	35.15
		45	41	2916	.69	.57	530	34.29

*Factor × typewritten pages = book pages   **Word = 5.5 characters

Register 1 = type body (size plus leading)
Register 2 = characters per pica (342/alphabet length)
Register 3 = type measure in picas and tenths
Register 4 = depth of page in picas and tenths
Register 5 = 100,000
Register 6 = 2025 (elite characters per manuscript page)
Register 7 = 1675 (pica characters per manuscript page)
Register 8 = (used by program for characters per page)
Register 9 = (used by program for lines per page)

The Program

Fix 1 decimal place for the display
Recall-4 × 12/Recall-1 = STOP   (*note lines per page*)
Store-9   Fix 0 decimal place
Recall-2 × Recall-3 × Recall-9 = STOP   (*note characters per page*)

Store-8   Fix 2 decimal places
Recall-8/Recall-6 = make reciprocal   STOP   (*note elite factor*)
Recall-8/Recall-7 = make reciprocal   STOP   (*note pica factor*)
Fix 0 decimal place
Recall-8/5.5 = STOP   (*note words per page*)
Fix 2 decimal places
Recall-5/Recall-8 = STOP   (*note text pages per 100,000 characters ms.*)
(*User enters new data in Reg. 1 or 2 or 3, as required for
  the table, and then presses R/S key.*)
Program resets to beginning.

In use

1. Decide what values of body, characters per pica, measure, and page depth the table is to cover. See the sample table for how values and columns are arranged.
2. Enter the program into calculator memory.
3. Store initial values in Regs. 1–7. (Other values may be used, of course, for elite and pica page character counts. The values given above allow about 1 1/8″ margins all around double-spaced pages.)
4. Start the program at the beginning by Reset.
5. Key six R/S and note the answers displayed. R/S: display shows lines per page of type.* R/S: display shows characters per page of type. R/S: display shows elite typewriter factor (× ms. pp. = book pp.). R/S: display shows pica typewriter factor (×ms. pp. = book pp.). R/S: display shows words per page of type. R/S: display shows type pages per 100,000 characters ms.
6. Repeat the above for each line of the desired table, noting the results. *At least* one value in Regs. 1–4 will have to be changed every line, because Reg. 4 changes every line. (It is best to fill out the first three columns of the table before starting to run the program, as a guide to changing the values in the registers.) Change the register values before starting the next cycle (i.e., after noting the last value in each line).
7. A number of special purpose tables can be generated in a short time for type and page sizes commonly used. As in the sample, each table is for a specific range of characters per pica (or alphabet length, which is essentially the same thing.) A range of .1 characters per pica should be a maximum. (See also Appendix B.)

---

*The program retains any fraction of a line, so that the user may decide to include or drop the extra line (by simply keying the integer into the display.) For example, in the first line of the sample table, the "lines" will appear as 46.9. The user *keys* 47 to indicate the extra line is accepted, or 46 if it is not.

3. TEXT FITTING OPTIONS.   *The adjustment of text specifications to typeset a given number of characters in a defined rectangular area such as a page.*

Note: This program solves for the somewhat complex problem type "C" as noted in the introduction. It can do the approximations faster than can be done via the tables. More importantly, it can use the fine fractional increments available in many modern composition systems (e.g., tenths of points for type body, width, depth, size, 1/100 em letterspacing or kerning, and so on). These require tables too large to be practical, except when special tables are defined for special needs.

The program uses the greatest integer number of lines that will fit into a given depth. Hence, when the most accurate results are required, set the depth to an even number of proposed lines. (See Table 5.)

Because it is desirable to have a form to record the assumed values and the results obtained, a sample is provided here.

TEXT FITTING OPTIONS

Area or page _____ Trimmed size _____

Type face_____ Source _____

Reg. 0 (target chars)_____ Reg. 3 Alphabet length, pts._____

Reg. 1 Width in points_____ Reg. 4 Type body, pts._____

Reg. 2 Depth in points_____ Reg. 5 10/10 pt al. length_____

Target chars.	(Ltr.#)	A/L	Size (set)	Body	Area chars.	Chars. sq. pi.

Register 1 = width of typesetting area in points
Register 2 = depth of typesetting area in points
Register 3 = lower case alphabet length in points note that this can include any adjustments for altered set width (use the value for the set width size), or for full-text kerning or letter spacing (add or subtract from the alphabet length 26 × the increment in points).
Register 4 = type body (size plus leading) in points and tenths
Register 5 = 10 divided by the 10-point alphabet length of type being used

Register 6 = (used by program for area characters)
Register 7 = (used by program for characters per pica)
Register 8 = (used by program for lines deep)
Register 9 = (used by program for characters per line)

The program

Fix 1 decimal place for the display
Recall-3 STOP   (*note alphabet length being used, and change it if desired*)
Store-3 × Recall-5 = STOP   (*note type size being used, which may
    be a fraction since it is controlled by alphabet length*)
Recall-4 STOP   (*note type body being used, and change it if desirable
    to change the leading*) Store-4   Recall-2/Recall-4 =
Take integer part only and Store-8
342/Recall-3 = (*characters per pica*) Store-7
× (Recall-1/12) = (*characters per line*) Store-9
× Recall-8 = (*area characters*)   Fix 0 decimals for display
STOP   (*note characters that can be set in the given area and
    compare to target; decide on changes to be made in alphabet length
    and leading as they next come up, as noted above*)
Store-6/(Recall-1 × Recall-2/144) = (*characters per square pica*)
Fix 2 decimal places for the display   STOP   (*note characters per square pica*)
Program resets to the beginning.

In use

1. Decide area width and depth for typesetting, and decide which values of alphabet length and type body will be used to start with. (Alphabet length value controls all aspects of face, size, set, and kerning or letterspacing of full text.)
2. Enter the program into calculator memory.
3. Store initial values in Regs. 1–5.
4. Start program at the beginning by keying Reset.
5. Key R/S five times per cycle.
    R/S: display shows current alphabet length in points. (To change, key the new value here. It will be stored automatically in Reg. 3.)
    R/S: display shows current size in points (may be fractional, following alphabet length, and small errors may be disregarded since this is for general information only, the exact value being the alphabet length).
    R/S: display shows current type body in points and tenths. (To change, key the new value here. It will be stored automatically in Reg. 4.)
    R/S: display shows current characters for the given area.
    R/S: display shows current characters per square pica.
6. Repeat the above cycle, varying the values of Regs. 3 and 4, as seems best, simply by *rekeying* them to the desired new values when they appear in the display at R/S #1 and #3. Reg. 1 and 2 may also be changed at any time if required. Note: Type size displayed is an approximation; changing it will have no effect on the program. To change size, change the alphabet length.

7. The user decides what changes to make in alphabet length (Reg. 3) and type body (Reg. 4) when the current characters that can be set within the given area are compared to a target (which may be stored for convenience in Reg. 0). When the results are satisfactorily "on target," the program has served its purpose. If the results are properly recorded on a form such as the one shown, many optional settings can be preserved for consideration. Immediately after each line of information is obtained, three pieces of information are available if needed: (1) characters per pica by keying Recall-7, (2) lines per area by Recall-8, and (3) characters per line by Recall-9.

8. If the alphabet length includes any set changes or text letterspacing, the size shown will be the *set size*. If the size is wanted as accurately as possible, for a range of sizes, change the value in Reg. 5 every 1–2 points, to exactly the value for the size being calculated. (Key: (Size)/(its A/L)=store-5.)

4. TO FIT A GIVEN NUMBER OF CHARACTERS INTO A GIVEN NUMBER OF SQUARE PICAS, BY VARYING SIZE AND LEADING

Note that because this program uses square picas rather than simple width and depth (as in #3 above), it can be used to fit irregular shapes and runarounds, as well as rectangular shapes. For example, to modify a rectangular shape by an irregular runaround, first find the square picas in the regular area. Then subtract the area required for the runaround (found by putting a piece of six-to-the-inch graph paper over the runaround shape required, and counting the squares). See nonrectangular areas in the introduction.

Because it is handy, although not required, to have a printer for this program, it will be given in two versions: with no printer and with printer.

Register 1 = given number of characters to be set
Register 2 = given square picas of area
Register 3 = alphabet length
Register 4 = type size/its alphabet length
Register 5 = type body
Register 6 = (used by the program)
Register 7 = (used by the program)
Register 8 = (contains required characters per square pica)
Register 9 = (contains actual characters per square pica)

The program, with no printer

Fix 1 decimal for the display
Recall-1/Recall-2 = STOP   (*shows required characters per square pica*)
Store-8   342/Recall-3   STOP   (*shows alphabet length* **which can be changed to adjust the type size or set.** *Just key the new value here.*)
Store-3 = (*characters per pica*)   Store-6
Recall-3 × Recall-4 = STOP   (*shows new size*)
Recall-6/12 = Store-6   144/Recall-5
STOP (*shows type body,* **which can be changed.** *Just key the new values here.*)
Store-5 = × Recall-6 = Store-9
Fix 2 decimals for the display
STOP   (*shows the actual characters per square pica, to compare with the first figure, the required value in line 2 above.*)
Program resets to the beginning.

The program, with printer

Fix 1 decimal for the display
Recall-1/Recall-2 = PRINT   (*the required characters per square pica*)
Store-8   342/Recall-3   STOP   (*the display shows the alphabet length,* **which can be changed to adjust the size or set.** *Just key the new value here.*)
Store-3   PRINT   (*the alphabet length, as changed if changed*)
= Store-6   Recall-3 × Recall-4 =   PRINT   (*new size*)
Recall-6/12 = Store-6   144/Recall-5

STOP (*display shows type body*, **which can be changed**. *Just key the new value here.*)
Store-5 PRINT (*type body, as changed if changed*)
= × Recall-6 = Store-9
Fix 2 decimal places for the display
PRINT (*actual characters per square pica, to compare with the first figure printed, the required value*)
Advance the paper 1 line Program resets to the beginning.

In use

1. Enter the program into the calculator memory.
2. Store the values required in Regs. 1 and 2.
3. Decide on initial trial values for Regs. 3, 4, and 5, and store them. (The value for Reg. 4 is obtained by using any typeface and size to correspond with the alphabet length in Reg. 3.)
4. Start the program at the beginning by keying Reset.
5. Key R/S five times per cycle if no printer is used, (twice per cycle is necessary using the printer). With no printer, these five values come up on the display:
   a. Required characters per square pica (*just a reminder*)
   b. Alphabet length (*changed as necessary*)
   c. Type size current (*do not change, it has no effect*)
   d. Type body current (*changed as necessary*)
   e. Actual characters per square pica (*for current b and d*)
   If you are using a printer, the program only stops on "b," the alphabet length, and "d," the type body, so that you can redefine them as seems best to make the actual characters per square pica conform to what is required. All the other values are simply printed out by the program.
   Note that (either with or without printer) this method makes it possible for the designer's judgment to do the adjusting and optimizing. Then it provides immediate knowledge of the results. Because design judgment are *required*, in respect to whether size (or set) or body should be modified in any given circumstance, no other system of adjustment or automatic optimization is practical.
   Printer output is shown below:

```
Required c.s.p.   4. 0      PRT
A/length        114. 0      PRT
Size              9. 0      PRT
Body              9. 5      PRT
Actual c.s.p.   3. 79      PRT

                  4. 0      PRT
                114. 0      PRT
                  9. 0      PRT
Body modified     9. 0      PRT
                  4. 00     PRT
```

6. Either with or without printer, the user simply keeps pressing R/S, and modifying alphabet length and/or type body until satisfaction is obtained. Note that (if the original area does not include a runaround) any given area can have many shapes, of rectangular width × depth.

5. "CASTOFF PLUS". *Provides user-designed adjustments and options that make possible desirable book length alternatives, or closer fitting of press forms. Consider the form shown here.*

The purpose of this form is to enable you to evaluate possible alternative text settings of your choosing, in relation to book length and even forms. Text length, of course, is adjusted in four ways:

1. Increase type body by leading
   Decrease type body by leading*
2. Use a more condensed type (with increased characters per pica)*
   Use a more expanded type (with decreased characters per pica)

3. Increase the measure (width)*
   Decrease the measure
4. Increase the page depth*
   Decrease the page depth   (Starred factors save pages)

BASIC DESIGN SPECIFICATIONS, AND CHARACTER COUNT OF MANUSCRIPT:

1. Type body (include "lead")   _____
2. Text type   _____
   Characters per pica   _____
3. Type measure (____cols)   _____
4. Page depth (picas)   _____
5. Characters in Ms. (text)   _____
   (If "by chapter," list over)

6. Total non-text pages: _____
   Front matter pp   _____
   Back matter pp   _____
   Number of pictures   _____
   Size of pix (1/10 pg)   avg. _____
   Captions   _____
   Extra display in book   _____

	DESIRED ADJUSTMENTS			Lines per page	Chars. per page	Text only	Total pages	32s	Blank	% Text + or −
	BODY	CH/PI	MEAS.	DEPTH							
	(None — basic design)									———
A											
B											
C											
D											
E											
F											

Typeface for CH/PI used above: (   ) _____   (   ) _____

Register 0 = (used by operator to store the text pages resulting from a "basic" design, to which other results are compared)

Register 1 = type body in points and tenths

Register 2 = characters per pica (342/alphabet length)

Register 3 = measure in picas and tenths

Register 4 = page depth in picas and tenths

Register 5 = characters in manuscript (text setting only)

Register 6 = total nontext pages, estimated

Register 7 = (used by program for characters per page)

Register 8 = (used by program for text pages)

Register 9 = (used by program for lines per text page)

The program

Fix 0 decimal places for the display

Recall-4 × 12/Recall-1 = (*lines per page*)   Make it an integer   Store-9

STOP   *(note lines per page on form)*

Recall-2 × Recall-3 × Recall-9 = *(characters per page)*   Store-7

STOP   *(note characters per page on the form)*

Recall-5/Recall-7 =   make it an integer   + 1 = *(text pages)*   Store-8

STOP   *(note text pages on form. Store only the first or basic-design value in Reg. 0)*   + Recall-6 = *(total pages in book)*

STOP   *(note total pages on form)*/32 = Store-7

make it an integer   + 1 = *(32 page forms)*

STOP   *(note number of 32 page forms)*   Recall-7

take fractional part only   × 32 − 32 =   change the sign   *(blank pages)*

STOP   *(note the number of blank pages required on the form)*

Recall-8/Recall-0   − 1 = *(percent of change from the design-reference pages in Reg. 0)*   Fix 2 decimal places for display

STOP   *(note percent of change from the reference set)*

Program resets to the beginning.

In use

1. To understand how the program operates, consider the form provided. Note on the form (1–6) the specifications chosen for the design-reference set of specifications. These are the "ideal" set to which other options will be compared: type body, characters per pica, measure, page depth, characters in the manuscript, and nontext pages.
2. Enter the program into calculator memory.
3. Store the initial design-reference values in Regs. 1–6.
4. Start the program at the beginning by keying Reset.
5. Key seven R/S.
   R/S: display shows lines per page, to be noted on the form.
   R/S: display shows characters per page, to be noted.
   R/S: display shows text pages, to be noted (store pages for the basic design in Reg. 0).*
   R/S: display shows total pages, to be noted.
   R/S: display shows number of 32-page forms, to be noted.
   R/S: display shows number of blank pages included, to be noted.
   R/S: display shows percent of change in text pages from the design-reference result stored in Reg. 0.
6. Having noted the results shown at the last three R/S's, decide what changes in specifications for type body, characters per pica, measure, and page depth will be likely to produce a more favorable result, or a result possibly worth considering. Make the changes, before starting the next cycle, by entering new values in Regs. 1–4. Any values that can be expressed as decimals are acceptable.
7. Repeat steps 5 and 6 until a satisfactory combination of specifications has been found, or until a reasonable number of options have been investigated. In many modern composition systems, the possible options within traditional limits of page size and type size and leading are nearly endless. It is thus necessary to consider alternatives with care, even though results can be quickly obtained by the program.

*If there is a zero value in Reg. 0, an error condition will result at the last R/S.

6. TO DETERMINE A TYPE SIZE TO FIT DISPLAY NEEDS. *Find the alphabet length of a type size (and style) that will set a certain approximate number of characters to a certain number of picas wide (either in initial cap and lower case or in caps, with or without letterspacing).*

Register 1 = number of characters to be set
Register 2 = width to be set in picas and tenths
Register 3 = letterspacing in points (if zero, enter zero)
Register 4 = (used by the program to store the answer in points)

The program

Fix 1 decimal place for the display
342/(Recall-1/(Recall-2 − (Recall-3 × Recall-1/12))) =
(*answer in points*) Store-4   /12 = STOP
(*displays answer in picas and tenths*)   Program resets to beginning.

In use

1. If the program is to be used for all caps, substitute the value 355 for the value 342 in the second line.
2. Enter the program into calculator memory.
3. Store the proper values in Regs. 1, 2, and 3.
4. Start the program at the beginning by pressing the Reset.
5. Press the R/S key, and the answer will appear in the display.
6. Note the answer (*which is in picas of alphabet length*, to make measurement easy), and then find the nearest style and size by measuring lower case alphabets. If the answer is wanted in points, simply key Recall-4, and it will be given in the display.
7. Repeat the procedure as desired, changing values in the registers as necessary.

ABCDEFGHIJKLMNOPQRSTUVWXYZ
abcdefghijklmnopqrstuvwxyz1234567890

ABCDEFGHIJKLMNOPQRSTUVWXYZ
abcdefghijklmnopqrstuvwxyz1234567890

ABCDEFGHIJKLMNOPQRSTUVWXYZ
abcdefghijklmnopqrstuvwxyz1234567890

ABCDEFGHIJKLMNOPQRSTUVWXYZ
abcdefghijklmnopqrstuvwxyz1234567890

ABCDEFGHIJKLMNOPQRSTUVWXYZ
abcdefghijklmnopqrstuvwxyz1234567890

ABCDEFGHIJKLMNOPQRSTUVWXYZ
abcdefghijklmnopqrstuvwxyz1234567890

7. TO DETERMINE TYPE SIZE, IN 32NDS OF AN INCH (OR POINTS) OF CAP HEIGHT. *Finds cap height in 32nds to set a certain number of characters, initial cap and lower case, to a certain width in picas.*

This is used for typositor style composition, using: a) the alphabet length in points of a sample alphabet, b) the cap height in points of the same sample alphabet, c) the number of characters to be set, and d) the proposed width of setting in picas.

Register 1 = lower case (or capitals) alphabet length of a sample alphabet in points (any size, but largest available, for accuracy)
Register 2 = cap height of the same sample alphabet in points
Register 3 = number of characters to be set
Register 4 = width of proposed setting in picas and tenths

The program

Fix 1 decimal place for the display
Recall-1/Recall-2 = (*ratio of alphabet length to cap height*)
Store-5   342/(Recall-3/Recall-4) = (*result*)   /Recall-5 =
(*answer, in points*) Store-6   ×.442 = STOP   (*answer, in 32nds-inch, is noted*)
Program resets to beginning.

In use

1. If the program is to be used for all caps, substitute the value 355 for 342 in the third line.
2. Enter the program into calculator memory.
3. Store the proper values in Regs. 1, 2, 3, and 4.
4. Start the program at the beginning by pressing the Reset.
5. Press the R/S key and the answer appears in the display.
6. Note the cap height is given in 32nds of an inch. If it is wanted in points, key Recall-6, and it will appear in the display.
7. Repeat as necessary, changing the values in Regs. 1–4.

Note that the answers are necessarily somewhat approximate, especially if only a few letters are involved or if caps and lower case are used instead of initial cap and lower case.

abcdefghijklmnopqrstuvwxyz
ABCDEFGHIJKLMNOPQRSTUVWXYZ
1234567890

8. LENGTH OF LINE IS GIVEN, BUT CHARACTERS IN COPY AND THE TYPE SIZE VARY. *This constructs a table to find the (approximate) size and the exact alphabet length to set varying numbers of characters to a given measure.*

Register 1 = line measure (constant)
Register 2 = characters to be set (will be incremented by 1)
Register 3 = type size/alphabet length of same size
Register 4 = (used by program for current alphabet length)
Register 5 = (used by program for current type size)

The program

Fix 0 decimal places for display
342/(Recall-2/Recall-1) = Store-4
× Recall-3 = Store-5   Recall-2   STOP (*shows characters to be set*)
Recall-5   Fix 1 decimal place for display
STOP   (*shows approximate size, plus tenths*)   Recall-4
Fix 0 decimal places for display   STOP   (*shows alphabet length*)
Add 1 to value in Reg. 2   Program resets to the beginning.

In use

1. Enter the program into calculator memory.
2. Decide on the constant line measure, and store in Reg. 1. Decide on the initial number of characters to be set (the number that can be set in the measure with the largest size considered), and store in Reg. 2.
3. Decide the smallest size to be considered. Take the midsize between the largest and the smallest sizes. Divide that point size by its alphabet length, and store the result in Reg. 3. This will be used to find the approximate size, from the exact alphabet length. However, if you want to be as exact as possible about the sizes, you can recalculate the value for Reg. 3 every couple of sizes that you calculate for, instead of using the midpoint figure for all. This can be desirable because point size, in some systems, is not quite a true linear function of alphabet length.
4. Start the program at the beginning by keying Reset.
5. Key three R/S, and note the results.
   R/S: Note the current characters that fit in the line (the first value is the smallest since it will be incremented).
   R/S: Note the type size (approximate, which may include fractions).
   R/S: Note the alphabet length, which is exact (from this, you can check the exact size if that is required).
6. Key R/S again, which starts a new cycle and shows the current characters, incremented now by 1. Continue pressing R/S and noting the results in this way until the smallest size you want to consider has been noted.

This program makes it possible easily to construct a table for each common measure in a magazine or book. The table will show at a glance the size that will be required to set a given number of characters to fill each measure, e.g., for headings.

9. TYPEFACE AND SIZE (ALPHABET LENGTH) IS GIVEN, BUT LINE LENGTH AND NUMBER OF CHARACTERS VARY. *This constructs a table to find the line lengths in picas and tenths resulting from increasing the number of characters to be set, the type size (alphabet length) remaining constant.*

Register 1 = number of characters to be set (to be incremented by 1)
Register 2 = alphabet length in points (constant)

The program *The bracketed segment is optional. It translates the decimal portion of line lengths to points. Omit if not needed.*

Fix 0 decimal places for the display.
Recall-1 PAUSE   (*shows current number of characters for 1/2 second*)
/(342/Recall-2) = (*measure*)
Fix 1 decimal place for the display
STOP   (*note current number of characters, and the measure*)
[Take the fractional part only × 12 =   make it an integer
Fix 0 decimal places for the display
STOP   (*display shows points only, corresponding to the decimal portion of the measure value just given*)]
Add 1 to value of register 1   Program resets to the beginning.

In use

1. Enter the program into the calculator memory.
2. Decide on the constant alphabet length (points) and store in Reg. 2.
3. Decide on initial number of characters (to be incremented) and store in Reg. 1.
4. Start the program at the beginning by keying Reset.
5. Key R/S. The display shows the current number of characters to be set, for 1/2 second, then halts showing the measure in picas and tenths. (If the optional program segment is used, R/S can be keyed again to translate tenths of picas to points. When R/S is keyed yet again, the program goes on to reset to the beginning.)
6. Repeat step 4 until all line lengths to be considered have been noted. The simple table that results will enable you to tell at a glance how a given heading style will set. Such a table takes only a few minutes to construct, and it can be useful for common heading settings to which you often want to fit copy.

10. SOME SPACING UNIT CONVERSIONS

In the operations of modern composing equipment, the em space is divided into varying numbers of "relative units," 18 or 36 or 48 or 54 or 100 relative units per em. Because of this the various kinds of subtle spacing, such as are available on many machines, are difficult to calculate or specify since points are too gross a unit and the relative units are unfamiliar to the user. For example, full-text kerning or letterspacing is almost always done in very subtle spacing units, often relative units. For this type of specification, it is useful to relate the various relative units to points, which are more familiar.

Any calculator will do the conversions more easily than by hand, but for numerous conversions a table can easily be constructed for handy reference.

Formulas for converting relative units to points, and points to relative units, are all essentially the same.

Converting points to relative units

Points to 1/18 em units	(points × 18)/point size
Points to 1/100 em units	(points × 100)/point size
Points to 1/9 em units	(points × 9)/point size
Points to 1/36 em units	(points × 36)/point size
Points to 1/54 em units	(points × 54)/point size

In general, where R stands for the number of relative units per em, to convert points to relative units:

$$\text{Relative units} = (\text{points} \times R)/\text{point size}$$

A table can be constructed by storing an initial value for points to be converted (this is incremented) in Reg. 2. With point size in Reg. 1, the program would be:

Add 1 (*or any value*) to Reg. 2   Recall-2   PAUSE (*shows points*)
×R = /Recall-1 =   STOP (*shows relative units*)
Program resets to the beginning.

Converting relative units to points

1/18 em units to points	(point size × 1/18 em units)/18
1/100 em units to points	(point size × 1/100 em units)/100
1/54 em units to points	(point size × 1/54 em units)/54

And so on. In general (when R stands for the number of relative units per em), to convert relative units to points:

$$\text{Points} = (\text{point size} \times \text{relative units})/R$$

A short program to effect this conversion, with point size in Reg. 1 and any number of units being entered before running the program, would be:

×Recall-1/R =   STOP (*shows points*)   Resets to the beginning.

If desired, a table can be constructed by storing an initial value for relative units to be converted (this is incremented) in Reg. 2. With point size in Reg. 1, the program would be:

Add 1 (*or more*) to value in Reg. 2   Recall-2   PAUSE (*shows relative units*)
×Recall-1/ R=   STOP (*shows points*)
Program resets to the beginning.

Some other conversions

1/18 em units to 1/100 em units	1/18 em units×5.555
1/100 em units to 1/18 em units	1/100 em units/5.555
Points to inches	points×.0138
Inches to points	inches/.0138
1/16 inches to points	1/16 inches/.222
Points to 1/16 inches	points×.222
Points to millimeters	points×.3505
Millimeters to points	millimeters/.3505

The general form of a program to write a table for such simple functions, with the value on the above left being in Reg. 1 and the constant on the right being in Reg. 2, is as follows:

Add 1 to Reg. 1   Recall-1   PAUSE (*shows current incrementing value*)
×(or/) Recall-2=   STOP (*shows converted value*)
Resets to the beginning.

As an example, the table on page 90, converting points and millimeters, was generated using this program, starting with 0 in Reg. 1 and .3505 in Reg. 2:

Fix 1 decimal place for display
Add .5 to Reg. 1   Recall-1   PAUSE (*shows points*)
×Recall-2=fix 4 decimal places for display   STOP (*shows millimeters*)
Program resets to the beginning.

Regarding metric conversion for the printing industry, it may be noted that for everyday work any nonautomatic converting points and millimeters would be both tedious and error producing. However, it is relatively convenient to start with millimeters except for the unfamiliarity. Still, even in machines calibrated for metric, tenths and hundredths of millimeters would be required. The length of 1/10 millimeter is almost 3/10 of one point, which is not a fine enough unit of measure for modern composition. The 1/100 millimeter, .0286 point would appear to suffice.

APPENDIX B

A program in Basic to generate tailored tables of castoff results

As noted, especially for much modern typesetting equipment with subtle adjustments, complete tables of castoff options are impractical for anything but a small fraction of the combinations available, because the tables would be too unwieldy to consult. Although the tables in this book provide universal solutions to the general problems of copyfitting, more specifically tailored tables answering a particular range of publishing requirements may also be desirable on occasion.

The table for the calculator program #2 is very useful. But in many situations the range of options produced may be of considerably greater size than is practical to copy by hand, or even run on a calculator. Such an extensive table is an easy job for a computer, which today most publishing companies either own or have access to.

The program that follows is written in the widely used Basic language* and writes tailored tables to the user's specifications. It will run on home computers and time-sharing systems with little or no modification, and on any installation supporting Basic, with perhaps minor modifications such as any such system could easily make. For most purposes, line printer output is the most practical form, although typeset form might be easiest to consult.

For any publishing house using a specific set of trimmed sizes and having other specific uses or requirements, this kind of tailored table can save many hours of calculations, provide easily accessible information and analysis not obtainable by other means—and pay for this book many, many times over!

To use the program, simply decide what ranges of characters per pica, type body, measure, and page depth are to be considered, and what fractional units of these are to be the "steps" by which the program operates. For example, to produce the modest table that follows, in the range of 6″×9″ trim:

2.5 to 3.0 characters per pica by .1 steps
11 to 12 point type body by .5 steps
25.5 to 27.5 pica measure by .5 steps (1 column)
41 to 44 pica depth (text only) by 1.0 steps.

*Radio Shack Level II Basic, specifically.

This produces a small tailored table of 360 lines, 3240 entries, which will run even on a home computer in three or four minutes, far less on larger computers. Extending the body range to 13 points, and substituting more subtle incremental steps of .05, .25, .25, and .25 (available on much modern composing equipment), the table expands dramatically to 19,200 lines and 172,800 entries. This takes about two hours to run on a home computer, but a small fraction of that on a large unit. In any case, it illustrates the need to consider table size before having it run. Lines will be the product of the number of steps (inclusive) requested for each of the four elements.

Note that measure ("Meas.") will be column measure, if format is more than one column. Minor adjustment may be required for some tables, so that column heads print at convenient intervals.

```
90 REM * * TAILORED CASTOFF TABLES: S. RICE / A PROGRAM IN 'BASIC' (RADIO SHACK LEVEL II BASIC)
95 REM * * TO SEE RESULTS ON A SCREEN CHANGE LPRINT TO PRINT STATEMENTS IN LINES 380,390,410
100 CLEAR 100: CLS: PRINT STRING$(63,"-"):PRINT"THIS PROGRAM WRITES TAILORED CASTOFF TABLES"
110 PRINT"DESCRIBED IN 'TYPE-CASTER: UNIVERSAL COPYFITTING' BY S. RICE": PRINT STRING$(63,"-")
120 PRINT "* * S. RICE, 41 WEST 96 ST., N.Y.C. 10025   749-1449 * *":PRINT
130 INPUT"HIT ENTER TO CONTINUE";Z6
140 CLS:PRINT:PRINT"DESIRED RANGES AND INCREMENTS MUST BE ENTERED FOR 1) CHARACTERS PER PICA, 2)
 TYPE BODY, 3) MEASURE (AND NUMBER OF COLUMNS), & 4) PAGE DEPTH"
150 PRINT: PRINT"YOU CAN SEE A DEMO, INSTEAD OF ENTERING THE VALUES. DEMO VALUES: CH/PICA 2.5-3,
 (E.G. INCLUDES TIMES ROMAN) BY .1, TYPE BODY 11 TO 12 PT BY .5 PT, MEASURE 25.5 TO 27.5 PI BY ,
 5 PI (1 COL.) AND DEPTH 41 TO 44 PI BY 1.0 PI"
160 PRINT:PRINT"(NOTE:'FACTORS' X COPY PAGES = BOOK PAGES)"
170 PRINT:INPUT"TO SEE THE DEMO ONLY ENTER 'D', ELSE ENTER 'N'";X1$
180 IF X1$="D" THEN C1=2.5:C2=3.0:C3=.1:B1=11:B2=12:B3=.5:M1=25.5:M2=27.5:M3=.5:M4=1:D1=41:D2=44
:D3=1.0:C=C1
190 A$="##.#":B$="##":C$="####":D$=".##":E$="###":F$="##.##":E1=2025 :P1=1675
200 IF X1$<>"D" THEN GOSUB 430
210 FOR C=C1 TO C2 STEP C3
220   GOSUB 380
230   FOR B=B1 TO B2 STEP B3
240    FOR M=M1 TO M2 STEP M3
250     FOR D=D1 TO D2 STEP D3
260      L= INT((12*D+.25*B)/B)*M4 :REM ALLOWS 1/4 LINE EXTRA
270      G=INT(C*M*L)
280      E=INT(100*(1/(G/E1))+.5)/100
290      P=INT(100*(1/(G/P1))+.5)/100
300      W=INT(G/5.5+.5)
310      T=INT(100*(100000/G)+.5)/100
320      GOSUB 410
330     NEXT D,M
340    LPRINT" "
350    REM * * INPUT "HIT ENTER TO CONTINUE";Z9: GOSUB 380: REM OMIT INITIAL 'REM * *' WHEN VIEWI
NG RESULTS ON SCREEN INSTEAD OF USING PRINTER
360 NEXT B,C
370 END
380 CLS: LPRINT" ":LPRINT M4;"COLUMN";"   CHARS/PI=";C:LPRINT STRING$(63,"-"): LPRINT TAB(21)"LI
NES";TAB(28)"CHARS";TAB(35)"ELITE";TAB(42)"PICA";TAB(48)"WORDS";TAB(56)"TEXT PP"
390 LPRINT TAB(0)"BODY";TAB(8)"MEAS.";TAB(15)"DEEP";TAB(21)"PAGE";TAB(28)"PAGE";TAB(35)"FACT.";T
AB(42)"FACT.";TAB(48)"BK PG";TAB(56)"100M CH" :LPRINT STRING$(63,"-")
400 RETURN
410 LPRINT TAB(0)B;TAB(7)M;TAB(14)D;TAB(21)L;TAB(27)G;TAB(34)E;TAB(41)P;TAB(48)W;TAB(56)T
420 RETURN
430 CLS:INPUT "FOR CHARACTERS PER PICA, ENTER 1) LOWEST VALUE, 2) HIGHEST VALUE, 3) SIZE OF STEP
 TO BE USED (SEPARATE BY COMMAS),";C1,C2,C3
440 PRINT:INPUT "FOR TYPE BODY, ENTER 1) LOWEST VALUE (POINTS AND TENTHS) 2) HIGHEST VALUE, 3) S
IZE OF STEP TO BE USED (SEPARATE BY COMMAS);"B1,B2,B3
450 PRINT:INPUT "FOR TYPE MEASURE (NOT PAGE WIDTH, IF MULTI-COLUMN), ENTER 1) LOWEST VALUE (PICA
S AND TENTHS) 2) HIGHEST VALUE, 3) SIZE STEP TO BE USED (SEPARATE BY COMMAS), 4) NUMBER OF COLU
MNS,";M1,M2,M3,M4
460 PRINT:INPUT "FOR TEXT PAGE DEPTH, ENTER 1) LOWEST VALUE, (PICAS AND TENTHS) 2) HIGHEST VALU
E, 3) SIZE STEP TO BE USED (SEPARATE BY COMMAS),";D1,D2,D3
470 C=C1
480 RETURN
```

APPENDIX C
Table 6   Some fitting options for the 6" × 9" trimmed size (An example of a tailored table. See Appendix B)

BODY	MEAS.	DEEP	LINES PAGE	CHARS PAGE	ELITE FACT.	PICA FACT.	WORDS BK PG	TEXT PP 100M CH
11	25.5	41	44	2805	.72	.6	510	35.65
11	25.5	42	46	2932	.69	.57	533	34.11
11	25.5	43	47	2996	.68	.56	545	33.38
11	25.5	44	48	3060	.66	.55	556	32.68
11	26	41	44	2860	.71	.59	520	34.97
11	26	42	46	2990	.68	.56	544	33.44
11	26	43	47	3055	.66	.55	555	32.73
11	26	44	48	3120	.65	.54	567	32.05
11	26.5	41	44	2915	.69	.57	530	34.31
11	26.5	42	46	3047	.66	.55	554	32.82
11	26.5	43	47	3113	.65	.54	566	32.12
11	26.5	44	48	3180	.64	.53	578	31.45
11	27	41	44	2970	.68	.56	540	33.67
11	27	42	47	3105	.65	.54	565	32.21
11	27	43	47	3172	.64	.53	577	31.53
11	27	44	48	3240	.63	.52	589	30.86
11	27.5	41	44	3025	.67	.55	550	33.06
11	27.5	42	46	3162	.64	.53	575	31.63
11	27.5	43	47	3231	.63	.52	587	30.95
11	27.5	44	48	3300	.61	.51	600	30.3
11.5	25.5	41	43	2741	.74	.61	498	36.48
11.5	25.5	42	44	2805	.72	.6	510	35.65
11.5	25.5	43	45	2868	.71	.58	521	34.87
11.5	25.5	44	46	2932	.69	.57	533	34.11
11.5	26	41	43	2795	.72	.6	508	35.78
11.5	26	42	44	2860	.71	.59	520	34.97
11.5	26	43	45	2925	.69	.57	532	34.19
11.5	26	44	46	2990	.68	.56	544	33.44
11.5	26.5	41	43	2848	.71	.59	518	35.11
11.5	26.5	42	44	2915	.69	.57	530	34.31
11.5	26.5	43	45	2981	.68	.56	542	33.55
11.5	26.5	44	46	3047	.66	.55	554	32.82
11.5	27	41	43	2902	.7	.58	528	34.46
11.5	27	42	44	2970	.68	.56	540	33.67
11.5	27	43	45	3037	.67	.55	552	32.93
11.5	27	44	46	3105	.65	.54	565	32.21
11.5	27.5	41	43	2956	.69	.57	537	33.83
11.5	27.5	42	44	3025	.67	.55	550	33.06
11.5	27.5	43	45	3093	.65	.54	562	32.33
11.5	27.5	44	46	3162	.64	.53	575	31.63
12	25.5	41	41	2613	.77	.64	475	38.27
12	25.5	42	42	2677	.76	.63	487	37.36
12	25.5	43	43	2741	.74	.61	498	36.48
12	25.5	44	44	2805	.72	.6	510	35.65
12	26	41	41	2665	.76	.63	485	37.52
12	26	42	42	2730	.74	.61	496	36.63
12	26	43	43	2795	.72	.6	508	35.78
12	26	44	44	2860	.71	.59	520	34.97
12	26.5	41	41	2716	.75	.62	494	36.82
12	26.5	42	42	2782	.73	.6	506	35.95
12	26.5	43	43	2848	.71	.59	518	35.11
12	26.5	44	44	2915	.69	.57	530	34.31
12	27	41	41	2767	.73	.61	503	36.14
12	27	42	42	2835	.71	.59	515	35.27
12	27	43	43	2902	.7	.58	528	34.46
12	27	44	44	2970	.68	.56	540	33.67
12	27.5	41	41	2818	.72	.59	512	35.49
12	27.5	42	42	2887	.7	.58	525	34.64
12	27.5	43	43	2956	.69	.57	537	33.83
12	27.5	44	44	3025	.67	.55	550	33.06

BODY	MEAS.	DEEP	LINES PAGE	CHARS PAGE	ELITE FACT.	PICA FACT.	WORDS BK PG	TEXT PP 100M CH
11	25.5	41	44	2917	.69	.57	530	34.28
11	25.5	42	46	3049	.66	.55	554	32.8
11	25.5	43	47	3116	.65	.54	567	32.09
11	25.5	44	48	3182	.64	.53	579	31.43
11	26	41	44	2974	.68	.56	541	33.62
11	26	42	46	3109	.65	.54	565	32.16
11	26	43	47	3177	.64	.53	578	31.48
11	26	44	48	3244	.62	.52	590	30.83
11	26.5	41	44	3031	.67	.55	551	32.99
11	26.5	42	46	3169	.64	.53	576	31.56
11	26.5	43	47	3239	.63	.52	589	30.88
11	26.5	44	48	3307	.61	.51	601	30.24
11	27	41	44	3088	.66	.54	561	32.38
11	27	42	46	3229	.63	.52	587	30.97
11	27	43	47	3299	.62	.51	600	30.31
11	27	44	48	3369	.6	.5	613	29.68
11	27.5	41	44	3146	.64	.53	572	31.79
11	27.5	42	46	3289	.62	.51	598	30.4
11	27.5	43	47	3360	.6	.5	611	29.76
11	27.5	44	48	3432	.59	.49	624	29.14
11.5	25.5	41	43	2850	.71	.59	518	35.09
11.5	25.5	42	44	2917	.69	.57	530	34.28
11.5	25.5	43	45	2983	.68	.56	542	33.52
11.5	25.5	44	46	3049	.66	.55	554	32.8
11.5	26	41	43	2906	.7	.58	528	34.41
11.5	26	42	44	2974	.68	.56	541	33.62
11.5	26	43	45	3042	.67	.55	553	32.87
11.5	26	44	46	3109	.65	.54	565	32.16
11.5	26.5	41	43	2962	.68	.57	539	33.76
11.5	26.5	42	44	3031	.67	.55	551	32.99
11.5	26.5	43	45	3100	.65	.54	564	32.26
11.5	26.5	44	46	3169	.64	.53	576	31.56
11.5	27	41	43	3018	.67	.56	549	33.13
11.5	27	42	44	3088	.66	.54	561	32.38
11.5	27	43	45	3158	.64	.53	574	31.67
11.5	27	44	46	3229	.63	.52	587	30.97
11.5	27.5	41	43	3074	.66	.54	559	32.53
11.5	27.5	42	44	3146	.64	.53	572	31.79
11.5	27.5	43	45	3217	.63	.52	585	31.08
11.5	27.5	44	46	3289	.62	.51	598	30.4
12	25.5	41	41	2718	.75	.62	494	36.79
12	25.5	42	42	2784	.73	.6	506	35.92
12	25.5	43	43	2850	.71	.59	518	35.09
12	25.5	44	44	2917	.69	.57	530	34.28
12	26	41	41	2771	.74	.6	504	36.09
12	26	42	42	2839	.71	.59	516	35.22
12	26	43	43	2906	.7	.58	528	34.41
12	26	44	44	2974	.68	.56	541	33.62
12	26.5	41	41	2824	.72	.59	513	35.41
12	26.5	42	42	2893	.7	.58	526	34.57
12	26.5	43	43	2962	.68	.57	539	33.76
12	26.5	44	44	3031	.67	.55	551	32.99
12	27	41	41	2878	.7	.58	523	34.75
12	27	42	42	2948	.69	.57	536	33.92
12	27	43	43	3018	.67	.56	549	33.13
12	27	44	44	3088	.66	.54	561	32.38
12	27.5	41	41	2931	.69	.57	533	34.12
12	27.5	42	42	3003	.67	.56	546	33.3
12	27.5	43	43	3074	.66	.54	559	32.53
12	27.5	44	44	3146	.64	.53	572	31.79

BODY	MEAS.	DEEP	LINES PAGE	CHARS PAGE	ELITE FACT.	PICA FACT.	WORDS BK PG	TEXT PP 100M CH
11	25.5	41	44	3029	.67	.55	551	33.01
11	25.5	42	46	3167	.64	.53	576	31.58
11	25.5	43	47	3235	.63	.52	588	30.91
11	25.5	44	48	3304	.61	.51	601	30.27
11	26	41	44	3088	.66	.54	561	32.38
11	26	42	46	3229	.63	.52	587	30.97
11	26	43	47	3299	.61	.51	600	30.31
11	26	44	48	3369	.6	.5	613	29.68
11	26.5	41	44	3148	.64	.53	572	31.77
11	26.5	42	46	3291	.62	.51	598	30.39
11	26.5	43	47	3362	.6	.5	611	29.74
11	26.5	44	48	3434	.59	.49	624	29.12
11	27	41	44	3207	.63	.52	583	31.18
11	27	42	46	3353	.6	.5	610	29.82
11	27	43	47	3426	.59	.49	623	29.19
11	27	44	48	3499	.58	.48	636	28.58
11	27.5	41	44	3266	.62	.51	594	30.62
11	27.5	42	46	3415	.59	.49	621	29.28
11	27.5	43	47	3489	.58	.48	634	28.66
11	27.5	44	48	3563	.57	.47	648	28.07
11.5	25.5	41	43	2960	.68	.57	538	33.78
11.5	25.5	42	44	3029	.67	.55	551	33.01
11.5	25.5	43	45	3098	.65	.54	563	32.28
11.5	25.5	44	46	3167	.64	.53	576	31.58
11.5	26	41	43	3018	.67	.56	549	33.13
11.5	26	42	44	3088	.66	.54	561	32.38
11.5	26	43	45	3158	.64	.53	574	31.67
11.5	26	44	46	3229	.63	.52	587	30.97
11.5	26.5	41	43	3076	.66	.54	559	32.51
11.5	26.5	42	44	3148	.64	.53	572	31.77
11.5	26.5	43	45	3219	.63	.52	585	31.07
11.5	26.5	44	46	3291	.62	.51	598	30.39
11.5	27	41	43	3134	.65	.53	570	31.91
11.5	27	42	44	3207	.63	.52	583	31.18
11.5	27	43	45	3280	.62	.51	596	30.49
11.5	27	44	46	3353	.6	.5	610	29.82
11.5	27.5	41	43	3192	.63	.52	580	31.33
11.5	27.5	42	44	3266	.62	.51	594	30.62
11.5	27.5	43	45	3341	.61	.5	607	29.93
11.5	27.5	44	46	3415	.59	.49	621	29.28
12	25.5	41	41	2822	.72	.59	513	35.44
12	25.5	42	42	2891	.7	.58	526	34.59
12	25.5	43	43	2960	.68	.57	538	33.78
12	25.5	44	44	3029	.67	.55	551	33.01
12	26	41	41	2878	.7	.58	523	34.75
12	26	42	42	2948	.69	.57	536	33.92
12	26	43	43	3018	.67	.56	549	33.13
12	26	44	44	3088	.66	.54	561	32.38
12	26.5	41	41	2933	.69	.57	533	34.09
12	26.5	42	42	3005	.67	.56	546	33.28
12	26.5	43	43	3076	.66	.54	559	32.51
12	26.5	44	44	3148	.64	.53	572	31.77
12	27	41	41	2988	.68	.56	543	33.47
12	27	42	42	3061	.66	.55	557	32.67
12	27	43	43	3134	.65	.53	570	31.91
12	27	44	44	3207	.63	.52	583	31.18
12	27.5	41	41	3044	.67	.55	553	32.85
12	27.5	42	42	3118	.65	.54	567	32.07
12	27.5	43	43	3192	.63	.52	580	31.33
12	27.5	44	44	3266	.62	.51	594	30.62

BODY	MEAS.	DEEP	LINES PAGE	CHARS PAGE	ELITE FACT.	PICA FACT.	WORDS BK PG	TEXT PP 100M CH
11	25.5	41	44	3141	.64	.53	571	31.84
11	25.5	42	46	3284	.62	.51	597	30.45
11	25.5	43	47	3355	.6	.5	610	29.81
11	25.5	44	48	3427	.59	.49	623	29.18
11	26	41	44	3203	.63	.52	582	31.22
11	26	42	46	3348	.6	.5	609	29.87
11	26	43	47	3421	.59	.49	622	29.23
11	26	44	48	3494	.58	.48	635	28.62
11	26.5	41	44	3264	.62	.51	593	30.64
11	26.5	42	46	3413	.59	.49	621	29.3
11	26.5	43	47	3487	.58	.48	634	28.68
11	26.5	44	48	3561	.57	.47	647	28.08
11	27	41	44	3326	.61	.5	605	30.07
11	27	42	46	3477	.58	.48	632	28.76
11	27	43	47	3553	.57	.47	646	28.15
11	27	44	48	3628	.56	.46	660	27.56
11	27.5	41	44	3387	.6	.49	616	29.52
11	27.5	42	46	3541	.57	.47	644	28.24
11	27.5	43	47	3618	.56	.46	658	27.64
11	27.5	44	48	3695	.55	.45	672	27.06
11.5	25.5	41	43	3070	.66	.55	558	32.57
11.5	25.5	42	44	3141	.64	.53	571	31.84
11.5	25.5	43	45	3212	.63	.52	584	31.13
11.5	25.5	44	46	3284	.62	.51	597	30.45
11.5	26	41	43	3130	.65	.54	569	31.95
11.5	26	42	44	3203	.63	.52	582	31.22
11.5	26	43	45	3275	.62	.51	595	30.53
11.5	26	44	46	3348	.6	.5	609	29.87
11.5	26.5	41	43	3190	.63	.53	580	31.35
11.5	26.5	42	44	3264	.62	.51	593	30.64
11.5	26.5	43	45	3338	.61	.5	607	29.96
11.5	26.5	44	46	3413	.59	.49	621	29.3
11.5	27	41	43	3250	.62	.52	591	30.77
11.5	27	42	44	3326	.61	.5	605	30.07
11.5	27	43	45	3401	.6	.49	618	29.4
11.5	27	44	46	3477	.58	.48	632	28.76
11.5	27.5	41	43	3310	.61	.51	602	30.21
11.5	27.5	42	44	3387	.6	.49	616	29.52
11.5	27.5	43	45	3464	.58	.48	630	28.87
11.5	27.5	44	46	3541	.57	.47	644	28.24
12	25.5	41	41	2927	.69	.57	532	34.16
12	25.5	42	42	2998	.68	.56	545	33.36
12	25.5	43	43	3070	.66	.55	558	32.57
12	25.5	44	44	3141	.64	.53	571	31.84
12	26	41	41	2984	.68	.56	543	33.51
12	26	42	42	3057	.66	.55	556	32.71
12	26	43	43	3130	.65	.54	569	31.95
12	26	44	44	3203	.63	.52	582	31.22
12	26.5	41	41	3042	.67	.55	553	32.87
12	26.5	42	42	3116	.65	.54	567	32.09
12	26.5	43	43	3190	.63	.53	580	31.35
12	26.5	44	44	3264	.62	.51	593	30.64
12	27	41	41	3099	.65	.54	563	32.27
12	27	42	42	3175	.64	.53	577	31.5
12	27	43	43	3250	.62	.52	591	30.77
12	27	44	44	3326	.61	.5	605	30.07
12	27.5	41	41	3156	.64	.53	574	31.69
12	27.5	42	42	3233	.63	.52	588	30.93
12	27.5	43	43	3310	.61	.51	602	30.21
12	27.5	44	44	3387	.6	.49	616	29.52

1 COLUMN   CHARS/PI= 2.9

BODY	MEAS.	DEEP	LINES PAGE	CHARS PAGE	ELITE FACT.	PICA FACT.	WORDS BK PG	TEXT PP 100M CH
11	25.5	41	44	3253	.62	.51	591	30.74
11	25.5	42	46	3401	.6	.49	618	29.4
11	25.5	43	47	3475	.58	.48	632	28.78
11	25.5	44	48	3549	.57	.47	645	28.18
11	26	41	44	3317	.61	.5	603	30.15
11	26	42	46	3468	.58	.48	631	28.84
11	26	43	47	3543	.57	.47	644	28.22
11	26	44	48	3619	.56	.46	658	27.63
11	26.5	41	44	3381	.6	.5	615	29.58
11	26.5	42	46	3535	.57	.47	643	28.29
11	26.5	43	47	3611	.56	.46	657	27.69
11	26.5	44	48	3688	.55	.45	671	27.11
11	27	41	44	3445	.59	.49	626	29.03
11	27	42	46	3601	.56	.47	655	27.77
11	27	43	47	3690	.55	.46	669	27.17
11	27	44	48	3758	.54	.45	683	26.61
11	27.5	41	44	3508	.58	.48	638	28.51
11	27.5	42	46	3668	.55	.46	667	27.26
11	27.5	43	47	3748	.54	.45	681	26.68
11	27.5	44	48	3827	.53	.44	696	26.13
11.5	25.5	41	43	3179	.64	.53	578	31.46
11.5	25.5	42	44	3253	.62	.51	591	30.74
11.5	25.5	43	45	3327	.61	.5	605	30.06
11.5	25.5	44	46	3401	.6	.49	618	29.4
11.5	26	41	43	3242	.62	.52	589	30.85
11.5	26	42	44	3317	.61	.5	603	30.15
11.5	26	43	45	3392	.6	.49	617	29.48
11.5	26	44	46	3468	.58	.48	631	28.84
11.5	26.5	41	43	3304	.61	.51	601	30.27
11.5	26.5	42	44	3381	.6	.5	615	29.58
11.5	26.5	43	45	3458	.59	.48	629	28.92
11.5	26.5	44	46	3535	.57	.47	643	28.29
11.5	27	41	43	3366	.6	.5	612	29.71
11.5	27	42	44	3445	.59	.49	626	29.03
11.5	27	43	45	3523	.57	.48	641	28.38
11.5	27	44	46	3601	.56	.47	655	27.77
11.5	27.5	41	43	3429	.59	.49	623	29.16
11.5	27.5	42	44	3508	.58	.48	638	28.51
11.5	27.5	43	45	3588	.56	.47	652	27.87
11.5	27.5	44	46	3668	.55	.46	667	27.26
12	25.5	41	41	3031	.67	.55	551	32.99
12	25.5	42	42	3105	.65	.54	565	32.21
12	25.5	43	43	3179	.64	.53	578	31.46
12	25.5	44	44	3253	.62	.51	591	30.74
12	26	41	41	3091	.66	.54	562	32.35
12	26	42	42	3166	.64	.53	576	31.59
12	26	43	43	3242	.62	.52	589	30.85
12	26	44	44	3317	.61	.5	603	30.15
12	26.5	41	41	3150	.64	.53	573	31.75
12	26.5	42	42	3227	.63	.52	587	30.99
12	26.5	43	43	3304	.61	.51	601	30.27
12	26.5	44	44	3381	.6	.5	615	29.58
12	27	41	41	3210	.63	.52	584	31.15
12	27	42	42	3288	.62	.51	598	30.41
12	27	43	43	3366	.6	.5	612	29.71
12	27	44	44	3445	.59	.49	626	29.03
12	27.5	41	41	3269	.62	.51	594	30.59
12	27.5	42	42	3349	.6	.5	609	29.86
12	27.5	43	43	3429	.59	.49	623	29.16
12	27.5	44	44	3508	.58	.48	638	28.51

1 COLUMN   CHARS/PI= 3

BODY	MEAS.	DEEP	LINES PAGE	CHARS PAGE	ELITE FACT.	PICA FACT.	WORDS BK PG	TEXT PP 100M CH
11	25.5	41	44	3365	.6	.5	612	29.72
11	25.5	42	46	3518	.58	.48	640	28.43
11	25.5	43	47	3595	.56	.47	654	27.82
11	25.5	44	48	3671	.55	.46	667	27.24
11	26	41	44	3431	.59	.49	624	29.15
11	26	42	46	3587	.56	.47	652	27.88
11	26	43	47	3665	.55	.46	666	27.29
11	26	44	48	3743	.54	.45	681	26.72
11	26.5	41	44	3497	.58	.48	636	28.6
11	26.5	42	46	3656	.55	.46	665	27.35
11	26.5	43	47	3736	.54	.45	679	26.77
11	26.5	44	48	3815	.53	.44	694	26.21
11	27	41	44	3563	.57	.47	648	28.07
11	27	42	46	3725	.54	.45	677	26.85
11	27	43	47	3806	.53	.44	692	26.27
11	27	44	48	3987	.52	.43	707	25.73
11	27.5	41	44	3629	.56	.46	660	27.56
11	27.5	42	46	3794	.53	.44	690	26.36
11	27.5	43	47	3877	.52	.43	705	25.79
11	27.5	44	48	3959	.51	.42	720	25.26
11.5	25.5	41	43	3289	.62	.51	598	30.4
11.5	25.5	42	44	3365	.6	.5	612	29.72
11.5	25.5	43	45	3442	.59	.49	626	29.05
11.5	25.5	44	46	3518	.58	.48	640	28.43
11.5	26	41	43	3353	.6	.5	610	29.82
11.5	26	42	44	3431	.59	.49	624	29.15
11.5	26	43	45	3509	.58	.48	638	28.5
11.5	26	44	46	3587	.56	.47	652	27.88
11.5	26.5	41	43	3418	.59	.49	621	29.26
11.5	26.5	42	44	3497	.58	.48	636	28.6
11.5	26.5	43	45	3577	.57	.47	650	27.96
11.5	26.5	44	46	3656	.55	.46	665	27.35
11.5	27	41	43	3482	.58	.48	633	28.72
11.5	27	42	44	3563	.57	.47	648	28.07
11.5	27	43	45	3644	.56	.46	663	27.44
11.5	27	44	46	3725	.54	.45	677	26.85
11.5	27.5	41	43	3547	.57	.47	645	28.19
11.5	27.5	42	44	3629	.56	.46	660	27.56
11.5	27.5	43	45	3712	.55	.45	675	26.94
11.5	27.5	44	46	3794	.53	.44	690	26.36
12	25.5	41	41	3136	.65	.53	570	31.89
12	25.5	42	42	3212	.63	.52	584	31.13
12	25.5	43	43	3289	.62	.51	598	30.4
12	25.5	44	44	3365	.6	.5	612	29.72
12	26	41	41	3197	.63	.52	581	31.28
12	26	42	42	3275	.62	.51	595	30.53
12	26	43	43	3353	.6	.5	610	29.82
12	26	44	44	3431	.59	.49	624	29.15
12	26.5	41	41	3259	.62	.51	593	30.68
12	26.5	42	42	3338	.61	.5	607	29.96
12	26.5	43	43	3418	.59	.49	621	29.26
12	26.5	44	44	3497	.58	.48	636	28.6
12	27	41	41	3320	.61	.5	604	30.12
12	27	42	42	3401	.6	.49	618	29.4
12	27	43	43	3482	.58	.48	633	28.72
12	27	44	44	3563	.57	.47	648	28.07
12	27.5	41	41	3382	.6	.5	615	29.57
12	27.5	42	42	3464	.58	.48	630	28.87
12	27.5	43	43	3547	.57	.47	645	28.19
12	27.5	44	44	3629	.56	.46	660	27.56

APPENDIX D
Forms to facilitate castoff

CHARACTERS PER LINE FROM CHARACTERS PER PICA

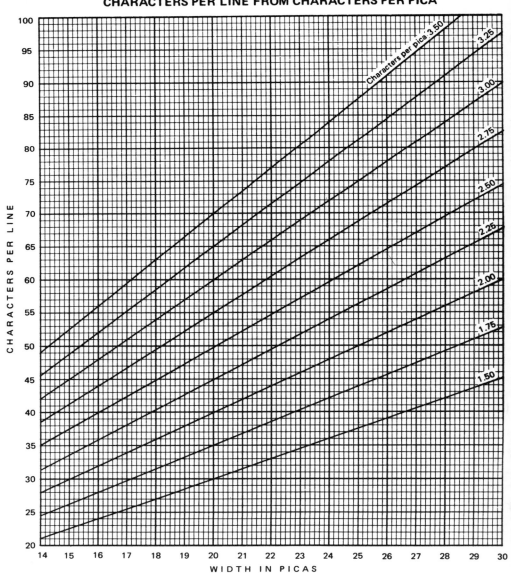

BOOK-LENGTH ESTIMATE FORM AND PAGE MAKEUP GUIDE

Date ___ / ___ / ___

Designer _____

Title _____ Author _____ Editor _____

1. Trimmed size_____×_____. Target total pages, excepting inserts (if any) _____
Ms. pages (text setting)_____× average chars. per ms. page_____= total chars. (text) _____
Total ms. characters secondary setting_____ *or* estimate % of ms: _____ % (See note, #9)
(Textheads, poetry, equations, outlines, etc. are counted in full pages of text, but see under #4 below.)
Editing complete?_____Illustrations total_____Half tone_____Line. Complete?_____
No. "PARTS"_____"CHAPTERS"_____
Elements to come _____

2. FRONT MATTER (circle blank pages)

PAGE	TO PAGE		NO. PGS.
_____	_____	Half title	_____
_____	_____	Card	_____
_____	_____	Frontisp.	_____
_____	_____	Title	_____
_____	_____	Copyright	_____
_____	_____	Dedication	_____
_____	_____	Epigraph	_____
_____	_____	Contents	_____
_____	_____	List of pix	_____
_____	_____	Foreword	_____
_____	_____	Preface	_____
_____	_____	Introduct.	_____
_____	_____	2nd Half T.	_____
_____	_____	_____	_____

Total front matter _____

3. BACK MATTER (estimated pages)

PAGE	TO PAGE		NO. PGS.
_____	_____	Appendix	_____
_____	_____	Notes	_____
_____	_____	Glossary	_____
_____	_____	Bibliography	_____
_____	_____	Index (1/30 Text)	_____
_____	_____	_____	_____
_____	_____	_____	_____

Total back matter_____ _____

4. MISCELLANEOUS (estimated pages) Pages
_____Halftones in text @_____/10 page = _____
_____Linecuts in text @_____/10 page = _____
Captions and spaces around pix, total _____
Tables and footnotes (if subtracted in #1) _____
Display space adjustment (space needed in book
compared to what is allowed in ms.) Total _____

Total miscellaneous _____

5. TOTAL NON-TEXT PAGES (front matter, back matter, and miscellaneous) _____

6. LENGTH ADJUSTMENT: If *no target* total length has been set for the book go to #9. Start with the most desirable typographic solution and modify as necessary for even forms in #11. But if a target has been set, in even signatures, adjust to it as follows:

	TARGET PAGES (per #1)	Revise 1	Revise 2	Revise 3	Revise 4
TARGET PAGES (per #1)	_____	_____	_____	_____	_____
Non Text pages (subtract)	_____	_____	_____	_____	_____
Target *text pages only*	_____	_____	_____	_____	_____

7. TARGET. Divide target *text* pages into characters in total text only (in #1) giving target characters per **text** page:

TARGET CHARS.	Revise 1	Revise 2	Revise 3	Revise 4
_____	_____	_____	_____	_____

8. Determine text settings having the target characters (or slightly more) per text page—*and* having acceptable combinations of typeface, leading, page width, and page depth. Note the acceptable options, available at compositor, in the form under #9. If **no** solutions are available or acceptable for the target characters per page (in #7) then go to #10 to adjust the target pages.
(NOTE: Compositor is _____Output device_____

(Continued on next page)

9. OPTIONS ACCEPTABLE AND AVAILABLE (Circle the option used on composition order)

	Option 1	Option 2	Option 3	Option 4	Option 5	Option 6
Characters per pica						
Typeface and/or no.						
Size and body						
Page width (text only)						
Page depth (text only)						
Characters per line						
Lines per page						
Characters per page						
Resulting text pages						
Adjustment for secondary*						
ADD: Total non-text pp. (#5)						
TOTAL PAGES EXCEPT INSERTS						

*If secondary was separately counted in #1 above, then add actual pages of secondary. If the secondary was estimated as percent of ms. text: (1) ignore if less than 10% (2) if more than 10% adjust by subtracting from "resulting text pages" of line above (1/5 × the percent secondary × resulting text pages).

10. If target characters per text page (in #7) are too *many* for any acceptable typographic solution then **increase** the target pages by adding one signature of minimum size (for this book, _____pp.). Then start again at #6. If target characters are too few for a good solution then **subtract** one signature.

11. ADJUSTMENT TO EVEN FORMS _____ 32s _____ 24s _____ 16s   OTHER: _____

	1st ESTIMATE	Revise-1	Revise-2	Revise-3	Revise-4	*FINAL*
DATE:	/ /	/ /	/ /	/ /	/ /	/ /
Front Matter						
Text & Secondary						
Misc. non-text (#4)						
Back matter (except index)						
Index						
Blanks						
TOTAL (EVEN SIGNATURES)						

12. INSERTS: ____groups of____pages. Placement follows pages: _____
For inserts without folios, sequence identification must be clear. **REVIEW PLACEMENT AT FINAL PAGING.**

13. TYPE PAGE AND MARGINS: Type page overall____×____picas. Space between text & running title____
Margins: head____gutter____. **NOT FINAL UNTIL CHECKED AT FINAL PAGING** (cf. lines per page + head margin).

APPENDIX E
Representative alphabet lengths and characters per pica values

The listings that follow are a general guide to fitting indexes for some popular type faces. But keep in mind that the same designs may fit rather differently on different machines (e.g., ITC designs,) and that modern typesetters allow modification of letter fitting on a system basis and also on a job basis. These listings designate the values normally implemented on the Linotron #202, using "regular" spacing of about 3 to em. Such spacing is wider than some typographers prefer, but it is still the most common industry usage.

In modern typesetting the only reliable indicator of how a face will fit is an alphabet length for a particular adjustment, from the target composition source. (Even these should be checked out when possible.) There is a 5–6% difference between Track 1 and Track 3 spacing on V-I-P machines; and CRTs can be controlled in even subtler ways in respect to letter fitting. The differences can be worth considering.

All this makes a forceful argument for checking alphabet length with the composition source, especially for critical jobs. And that is why Table 1 in this book is based on alphabet length (or characters per pica). It is the only basis for accurate castoff of modern composition.

In the tables that follow "AL/LENGTH" means alphabet length, "CHS/PI" means characters per pica, "CAP 'X'" means the height of the cap X in points, and "LC 'x'" means the height of the lower case x in points.

AVANT GARDE GOTHIC BOOK (LINOTRON #202)

SIZE	AL/LENGTH	CHS/PI	CAP'X'	LC'X'
6	80 PTS	4.28	4.5	3.3
6.5	87 PTS	3.94	4.9	3.6
7	93 PTS	3.66	5.2	3.8
7.5	100 PTS	3.41	5.6	4.1
8	107 PTS	3.2	6	4.4
8.5	114 PTS	3.01	6.3	4.6
9	120 PTS	2.84	6.7	4.9
9.5	127 PTS	2.69	7.1	5.2
10	134 PTS	2.56	7.5	5.5
10.5	140 PTS	2.43	7.8	5.7
11	147 PTS	2.32	8.2	6
11.5	154 PTS	2.22	8.6	6.3
12	161 PTS	2.13	9	6.6
12.5	167 PTS	2.04	9.3	6.8
13	174 PTS	1.96	9.7	7.1
13.5	181 PTS	1.89	10.1	7.4
14	188 PTS	1.82	10.5	7.7
15	16.7 PI	1.7	11.2	8.2
16	17.9 PI	1.6	11.9	8.7
17	19 PI	1.5	12.7	9.3
18	20.1 PI	1.42	13.4	9.8
19	21.2 PI	1.34	14.2	10.4
20	22.3 PI	1.28	14.9	10.9
21	23.5 PI	1.21	15.7	11.5
22	24.6 PI	1.16	16.4	12
23	25.7 PI	1.11	17.2	12.6
24	26.8 PI	1.06	17.9	13.1
25	27.9 PI	1.02	18.7	13.7
26	29.1 PI	.98	19.4	14.2
27	30.2 PI	.94	20.2	14.8
28	31.3 PI	.91	20.9	15.3
29	32.4 PI	.88	21.7	15.9
30	33.5 PI	.85	22.4	16.4
31	34.7 PI	.82	23.1	16.9
32	35.8 PI	.8	23.9	17.5
33	36.9 PI	.77	24.6	18
34	38 PI	.75	25.4	18.6
35	39.1 PI	.73	26.1	19.1
36	40.3 PI	.71	26.9	19.7
37	41.4 PI	.69	27.6	20.2
38	42.5 PI	.67	28.4	20.8
39	43.6 PI	.65	29.1	21.3
40	44.7 PI	.64	29.9	21.9
41	45.9 PI	.62	30.6	22.4
42	47 PI	.61	31.4	23
43	48.1 PI	.59	32.1	23.5
44	49.2 PI	.58	32.9	24.1
45	50.3 PI	.57	33.6	24.6
46	51.5 PI	.55	34.3	25.1
47	52.6 PI	.54	35.1	25.7
48	53.7 PI	.53	35.8	26.2
49	54.8 PI	.52	36.6	26.8
50	55.9 PI	.51	37.3	27.3
51	57.1 PI	.5	38.1	27.9
52	58.2 PI	.49	38.8	28.4
53	59.3 PI	.48	39.6	29
54	60.4 PI	.47	40.3	29.5
55	61.5 PI	.46	41.1	30.1
56	62.7 PI	.45	41.8	30.6
57	63.8 PI	.45	42.6	31.2
58	64.9 PI	.44	43.3	31.7
59	66 PI	.43	44.1	32.3
60	67.1 PI	.42	44.8	32.8
61	68.3 PI	.42	45.5	33.3
62	69.4 PI	.41	46.3	33.9
63	70.5 PI	.4	47	34.4
64	71.6 PI	.4	47.8	35
65	72.7 PI	.39	48.5	35.5
66	73.9 PI	.39	49.3	36.1
67	75 PI	.38	50	36.6
68	76.1 PI	.37	50.8	37.2
69	77.2 PI	.37	51.5	37.7
70	78.3 PI	.36	52.3	38.3
71	79.5 PI	.36	53	38.8
72	80.6 PI	.35	53.8	39.4

BASKERVILLE (LINOTRON #202)

SIZE	AL/LENGTH	CHS/PI	CAP'X'	LC'X'
6	79 PTS	4.33	4.1	2.7
6.5	86 PTS	3.99	4.4	2.9
7	92 PTS	3.7	4.7	3.1
7.5	99 PTS	3.46	5.1	3.3
8	106 PTS	3.24	5.4	3.5
8.5	112 PTS	3.05	5.8	3.8
9	119 PTS	2.88	6.1	4
9.5	126 PTS	2.72	6.4	4.2
10	132 PTS	2.59	6.8	4.4
10.5	139 PTS	2.46	7.1	4.7
11	146 PTS	2.35	7.4	4.9
11.5	152 PTS	2.25	7.8	5.1
12	159 PTS	2.15	8.1	5.3
12.5	166 PTS	2.07	8.5	5.5
13	172 PTS	1.99	8.8	5.8
13.5	179 PTS	1.91	9.1	6
14	186 PTS	1.84	9.5	6.2
15	16.6 PI	1.72	10.2	6.7
16	17.7 PI	1.61	10.8	7.1
17	18.8 PI	1.52	11.5	7.5
18	19.9 PI	1.43	12.2	8
19	21 PI	1.36	12.9	8.4
20	22.1 PI	1.29	13.5	8.9
21	23.2 PI	1.23	14.2	9.3
22	24.3 PI	1.17	14.9	9.8
23	25.4 PI	1.12	15.6	10.2
24	26.6 PI	1.07	16.2	10.6
25	27.7 PI	1.03	16.9	11.1
26	28.8 PI	.99	17.6	11.5
27	29.9 PI	.95	18.3	12
28	31 PI	.92	18.9	12.4
29	32.1 PI	.89	19.6	12.9
30	33.2 PI	.86	20.3	13.3
31	34.3 PI	.83	21	13.7
32	35.4 PI	.8	21.7	14.2
33	36.5 PI	.78	22.3	14.6
34	37.6 PI	.76	23	15.1
35	38.8 PI	.74	23.7	15.5
36	39.9 PI	.71	24.4	16
37	41 PI	.7	25	16.4
38	42.1 PI	.68	25.7	16.8
39	43.2 PI	.66	26.4	17.3
40	44.3 PI	.64	27.1	17.7
41	45.4 PI	.63	27.7	18.2
42	46.5 PI	.61	28.4	18.6
43	47.6 PI	.6	29.1	19.1
44	48.7 PI	.58	29.8	19.5
45	49.8 PI	.57	30.5	20
46	51 PI	.56	31.1	20.4
47	52.1 PI	.55	31.8	20.8
48	53.2 PI	.54	32.5	21.3
49	54.3 PI	.52	33.2	21.7
50	55.4 PI	.51	33.8	22.2
51	56.5 PI	.5	34.5	22.6
52	57.6 PI	.49	35.2	23.1
53	58.7 PI	.49	35.9	23.5
54	59.8 PI	.48	36.5	23.9
55	60.9 PI	.47	37.2	24.4
56	62.1 PI	.46	37.9	24.8
57	63.2 PI	.45	38.6	25.3
58	64.3 PI	.44	39.2	25.7
59	65.4 PI	.44	39.9	26.2
60	66.5 PI	.43	40.6	26.6
61	67.6 PI	.42	41.3	27
62	68.7 PI	.41	42	27.5
63	69.8 PI	.41	42.6	27.9
64	70.9 PI	.4	43.3	28.4
65	72 PI	.4	44	28.8
66	73.1 PI	.39	44.7	29.3
67	74.3 PI	.38	45.3	29.7
68	75.4 PI	.38	46	30.1
69	76.5 PI	.37	46.7	30.6
70	77.6 PI	.37	47.4	31
71	78.7 PI	.36	48	31.5
72	79.8 PI	.36	48.7	31.9

BODONI (LINOTRON #202)

SIZE	AL/LENGTH	CHS/PI	CAP'X'	LC'X'
6	74 PTS	4.62	4	2.3
6.5	80 PTS	4.26	4.3	2.5
7	86 PTS	3.96	4.7	2.7
7.5	93 PTS	3.69	5	2.9
8	99 PTS	3.46	5.3	3.1
8.5	105 PTS	3.25	5.7	3.3
9	111 PTS	3.07	6	3.5
9.5	118 PTS	2.91	6.3	3.7
10	124 PTS	2.76	6.7	3.9
10.5	130 PTS	2.63	7	4.1
11	136 PTS	2.51	7.3	4.3
11.5	142 PTS	2.4	7.7	4.5
12	149 PTS	2.3	8	4.7
12.5	155 PTS	2.21	8.3	4.9
13	161 PTS	2.12	8.7	5.1
13.5	167 PTS	2.04	9	5.3
14	174 PTS	1.97	9.3	5.5
15	15.5 PI	1.84	10	5.9
16	16.5 PI	1.72	10.7	6.2
17	17.6 PI	1.62	11.3	6.6
18	18.6 PI	1.53	12	7
19	19.6 PI	1.45	12.7	7.4
20	20.7 PI	1.38	13.3	7.8
21	21.7 PI	1.31	14	8.2
22	22.8 PI	1.25	14.7	8.6
23	23.8 PI	1.2	15.3	9
24	24.8 PI	1.15	16	9.4
25	25.9 PI	1.1	16.7	9.8
26	26.9 PI	1.06	17.3	10.1
27	27.9 PI	1.02	18	10.5
28	29 PI	.98	18.7	10.9
29	30 PI	.95	19.3	11.3
30	31 PI	.92	20	11.7
31	32.1 PI	.89	20.7	12.1
32	33.1 PI	.86	21.3	12.5
33	34.2 PI	.83	22	12.9
34	35.2 PI	.81	22.7	13.3
35	36.2 PI	.79	23.3	13.7
36	37.3 PI	.76	24	14
37	38.3 PI	.74	24.7	14.4
38	39.3 PI	.72	25.3	14.8
39	40.4 PI	.71	26	15.2
40	41.4 PI	.69	26.7	15.6
41	42.4 PI	.67	27.3	16
42	43.5 PI	.66	28	16.4
43	44.5 PI	.64	28.7	16.8
44	45.6 PI	.63	29.3	17.2
45	46.6 PI	.61	30	17.6
46	47.6 PI	.6	30.7	17.9
47	48.7 PI	.59	31.3	18.3
48	49.7 PI	.57	32	18.7
49	50.7 PI	.56	32.7	19.1
50	51.8 PI	.55	33.3	19.5
51	52.8 PI	.54	34	19.9
52	53.8 PI	.53	34.7	20.3
53	54.9 PI	.52	35.3	20.7
54	55.9 PI	.51	36	21.1
55	57 PI	.5	36.7	21.4
56	58 PI	.49	37.3	21.8
57	59 PI	.48	38	22.2
58	60.1 PI	.47	38.7	22.6
59	61.1 PI	.47	39.3	23
60	62.1 PI	.46	40	23.4
61	63.2 PI	.45	40.7	23.8
62	64.2 PI	.44	41.3	24.2
63	65.2 PI	.44	42	24.6
64	66.3 PI	.43	42.7	25
65	67.3 PI	.42	43.3	25.3
66	68.4 PI	.42	44	25.7
67	69.4 PI	.41	44.7	26.1
68	70.4 PI	.4	45.3	26.5
69	71.5 PI	.4	46	26.9
70	72.5 PI	.39	46.7	27.3
71	73.5 PI	.39	47.3	27.7
72	74.6 PI	.38	48	28.1

CALEDONIA (LINOTRON #202)

SIZE	AL/LENGTH	CHS/PI	CAP'X'	LC'X'
6	74 PTS	4.62	4.1	2.5
6.5	80 PTS	4.26	4.4	2.8
7	86 PTS	3.96	4.7	3
7.5	93 PTS	3.69	5.1	3.2
8	99 PTS	3.46	5.4	3.4
8.5	105 PTS	3.25	5.8	3.6
9	111 PTS	3.07	6.1	3.8
9.5	118 PTS	2.91	6.4	4
10	124 PTS	2.76	6.8	4.2
10.5	130 PTS	2.63	7.1	4.4
11	136 PTS	2.51	7.4	4.7
11.5	142 PTS	2.4	7.8	4.9
12	149 PTS	2.3	8.1	5.1
12.5	155 PTS	2.21	8.5	5.3
13	161 PTS	2.12	8.8	5.5
13.5	167 PTS	2.04	9.1	5.7
14	174 PTS	1.97	9.5	5.9
15	15.5 PI	1.84	10.2	6.4
16	16.5 PI	1.72	10.8	6.8
17	17.6 PI	1.62	11.5	7.2
18	18.6 PI	1.53	12.2	7.6
19	19.6 PI	1.45	12.9	8
20	20.7 PI	1.38	13.5	8.5
21	21.7 PI	1.31	14.2	8.9
22	22.8 PI	1.25	14.9	9.3
23	23.8 PI	1.2	15.6	9.7
24	24.8 PI	1.15	16.2	10.2
25	25.9 PI	1.1	16.9	10.6
26	26.9 PI	1.06	17.6	11
27	27.9 PI	1.02	18.3	11.4
28	29 PI	.98	18.9	11.9
29	30 PI	.95	19.6	12.3
30	31 PI	.92	20.3	12.7
31	32.1 PI	.89	21	13.1
32	33.1 PI	.86	21.7	13.5
33	34.2 PI	.83	22.3	14
34	35.2 PI	.81	23	14.4
35	36.2 PI	.79	23.7	14.8
36	37.3 PI	.76	24.4	15.2
37	38.3 PI	.74	25	15.7
38	39.3 PI	.72	25.7	16.1
39	40.4 PI	.71	26.4	16.5
40	41.4 PI	.69	27.1	16.9
41	42.4 PI	.67	27.7	17.4
42	43.5 PI	.66	28.4	17.8
43	44.5 PI	.64	29.1	18.2
44	45.6 PI	.63	29.8	18.6
45	46.6 PI	.61	30.5	19.1
46	47.6 PI	.6	31.1	19.5
47	48.7 PI	.59	31.8	19.9
48	49.7 PI	.57	32.5	20.3
49	50.7 PI	.56	33.2	20.7
50	51.8 PI	.55	33.8	21.2
51	52.8 PI	.54	34.5	21.6
52	53.8 PI	.53	35.2	22
53	54.9 PI	.52	35.9	22.4
54	55.9 PI	.51	36.5	22.9
55	57 PI	.5	37.2	23.3
56	58 PI	.49	37.9	23.7
57	59 PI	.48	38.6	24.1
58	60.1 PI	.47	39.2	24.6
59	61.1 PI	.47	39.9	25
60	62.1 PI	.46	40.6	25.4
61	63.2 PI	.45	41.3	25.8
62	64.2 PI	.44	42	26.2
63	65.2 PI	.44	42.6	26.7
64	66.3 PI	.43	43.3	27.1
65	67.3 PI	.42	44	27.5
66	68.4 PI	.42	44.7	27.9
67	69.4 PI	.41	45.3	28.4
68	70.4 PI	.4	46	28.8
69	71.5 PI	.4	46.7	29.2
70	72.5 PI	.39	47.4	29.6
71	73.5 PI	.39	48	30.1
72	74.6 PI	.38	48.7	30.5

CENTURY EXPANDED (LINOTRON #202)

SIZE	AL/LENGTH	CHS/PI	CAP'X'	LC'X'
6	78 PTS	4.38	4.4	2.9
6.5	85 PTS	4.05	4.7	3.1
7	91 PTS	3.76	5.1	3.3
7.5	98 PTS	3.5	5.5	3.6
8	104 PTS	3.28	5.8	3.8
8.5	111 PTS	3.09	6.2	4.1
9	117 PTS	2.92	6.5	4.3
9.5	124 PTS	2.76	6.9	4.5
10	130 PTS	2.63	7.3	4.8
10.5	137 PTS	2.5	7.6	5
11	143 PTS	2.39	8	5.2
11.5	150 PTS	2.28	8.4	5.5
12	156 PTS	2.19	8.7	5.7
12.5	163 PTS	2.1	9.1	6
13	169 PTS	2.02	9.4	6.2
13.5	176 PTS	1.94	9.8	6.4
14	183 PTS	1.87	10.2	6.7
15	16.3 PI	1.75	10.9	7.2
16	17.4 PI	1.64	11.6	7.6
17	18.5 PI	1.54	12.4	8.1
18	19.6 PI	1.46	13.1	8.6
19	20.7 PI	1.38	13.8	9.1
20	21.7 PI	1.31	14.5	9.5
21	22.8 PI	1.25	15.3	10
22	23.9 PI	1.19	16	10.5
23	25 PI	1.14	16.7	11
24	26.1 PI	1.09	17.4	11.4
25	27.2 PI	1.05	18.2	11.9
26	28.3 PI	1.01	18.9	12.4
27	29.4 PI	.97	19.6	12.9
28	30.4 PI	.94	20.3	13.3
29	31.5 PI	.9	21.1	13.8
30	32.6 PI	.87	21.8	14.3
31	33.7 PI	.85	22.5	14.8
32	34.8 PI	.82	23.3	15.3
33	35.9 PI	.79	24	15.7
34	37 PI	.77	24.7	16.2
35	38.1 PI	.75	25.4	16.7
36	39.2 PI	.73	26.2	17.2
37	40.2 PI	.71	26.9	17.6
38	41.3 PI	.69	27.6	18.1
39	42.4 PI	.67	28.3	18.6
40	43.5 PI	.66	29.1	19.1
41	44.6 PI	.64	29.8	19.5
42	45.7 PI	.62	30.5	20
43	46.8 PI	.61	31.2	20.5
44	47.9 PI	.6	32	21
45	49 PI	.58	32.7	21.5
46	50 PI	.57	33.4	21.9
47	51.1 PI	.56	34.2	22.4
48	52.2 PI	.55	34.9	22.9
49	53.3 PI	.53	35.6	23.4
50	54.4 PI	.52	36.3	23.8
51	55.5 PI	.51	37.1	24.3
52	56.6 PI	.5	37.8	24.8
53	57.7 PI	.49	38.5	25.3
54	58.8 PI	.49	39.2	25.7
55	59.8 PI	.48	40	26.2
56	60.9 PI	.47	40.7	26.7
57	62 PI	.46	41.4	27.2
58	63.1 PI	.45	42.1	27.6
59	64.2 PI	.44	42.9	28.1
60	65.3 PI	.44	43.6	28.6
61	66.4 PI	.43	44.3	29.1
62	67.5 PI	.42	45.1	29.6
63	68.5 PI	.42	45.8	30
64	69.6 PI	.41	46.5	30.5
65	70.7 PI	.4	47.2	31
66	71.8 PI	.4	48	31.5
67	72.9 PI	.39	48.7	31.9
68	74 PI	.39	49.4	32.4
69	75.1 PI	.38	50.1	32.9
70	76.2 PI	.37	50.9	33.4
71	77.3 PI	.37	51.6	33.8
72	78.3 PI	.36	52.3	34.3

FRUTIGER #45 (LINOTRON #202)

SIZE	AL/LENGTH	CHS/PI	CAP'X'	LC'X'
6	73 PTS	4.68	4.2	3.1
6.5	79 PTS	4.32	4.5	3.3
7	85 PTS	4	4.9	3.6
7.5	92 PTS	3.73	5.3	3.8
8	98 PTS	3.49	5.6	4.1
8.5	104 PTS	3.29	6	4.3
9	110 PTS	3.1	6.3	4.6
9.5	117 PTS	2.93	6.7	4.8
10	123 PTS	2.79	7	5.1
10.5	129 PTS	2.65	7.4	5.4
11	135 PTS	2.53	7.7	5.6
11.5	141 PTS	2.42	8.1	5.9
12	148 PTS	2.32	8.4	6.1
12.5	154 PTS	2.22	8.8	6.4
13	160 PTS	2.14	9.1	6.6
13.5	166 PTS	2.06	9.5	6.9
14	173 PTS	1.98	9.8	7.1
15	15.4 PI	1.85	10.5	7.7
16	16.4 PI	1.73	11.2	8.2
17	17.5 PI	1.63	11.9	8.7
18	18.5 PI	1.54	12.6	9.2
19	19.6 PI	1.46	13.3	9.7
20	20.6 PI	1.38	14	10.2
21	21.6 PI	1.32	14.7	10.7
22	22.7 PI	1.26	15.4	11.2
23	23.7 PI	1.2	16.1	11.7
24	24.7 PI	1.15	16.8	12.2
25	25.8 PI	1.11	17.5	12.8
26	26.8 PI	1.06	18.2	13.3
27	27.8 PI	1.02	18.9	13.8
28	28.9 PI	.99	19.6	14.3
29	29.9 PI	.95	20.3	14.8
30	31 PI	.92	21	15.3
31	32 PI	.89	21.7	15.8
32	33 PI	.86	22.4	16.3
33	34.1 PI	.84	23.1	16.8
34	35.1 PI	.81	23.8	17.3
35	36.1 PI	.79	24.5	17.9
36	37.2 PI	.77	25.2	18.4
37	38.2 PI	.75	25.9	18.9
38	39.3 PI	.73	26.6	19.4
39	40.3 PI	.71	27.3	19.9
40	41.3 PI	.69	28	20.4
41	42.4 PI	.67	28.7	20.9
42	43.4 PI	.66	29.4	21.4
43	44.4 PI	.64	30.1	21.9
44	45.5 PI	.63	30.8	22.4
45	46.5 PI	.61	31.5	23
46	47.5 PI	.6	32.2	23.5
47	48.6 PI	.59	32.9	24
48	49.6 PI	.57	33.6	24.5
49	50.7 PI	.56	34.3	25
50	51.7 PI	.55	35	25.5
51	52.7 PI	.54	35.7	26
52	53.8 PI	.53	36.4	26.5
53	54.8 PI	.52	37.1	27
54	55.8 PI	.51	37.8	27.5
55	56.9 PI	.5	38.5	28.1
56	57.9 PI	.49	39.2	28.6
57	58.9 PI	.48	39.9	29.1
58	60 PI	.48	40.6	29.6
59	61 PI	.47	41.3	30.1
60	62.1 PI	.46	42	30.6
61	63.1 PI	.45	42.7	31.1
62	64.1 PI	.44	43.4	31.6
63	65.2 PI	.44	44.1	32.1
64	66.2 PI	.43	44.8	32.6
65	67.2 PI	.42	45.5	33.2
66	68.3 PI	.42	46.2	33.7
67	69.3 PI	.41	46.9	34.2
68	70.3 PI	.41	47.6	34.7
69	71.4 PI	.4	48.3	35.2
70	72.4 PI	.39	49	35.7
71	73.5 PI	.39	49.7	36.2
72	74.5 PI	.38	50.4	36.7

GARAMOND #3 (LINOTRON #202)

SIZE	AL/LENGTH	CHS/PI	CAP'X'	LC'X'
6	67 PTS	5.1	3.7	2.3
6.5	73 PTS	4.7	4	2.5
7	78 PTS	4.36	4.3	2.7
7.5	84 PTS	4.06	4.6	2.9
8	90 PTS	3.81	4.9	3.1
8.5	96 PTS	3.58	5.2	3.3
9	101 PTS	3.38	5.5	3.5
9.5	107 PTS	3.2	5.8	3.6
10	113 PTS	3.03	6.1	3.8
10.5	118 PTS	2.89	6.4	4
11	124 PTS	2.75	6.7	4.2
11.5	130 PTS	2.63	7	4.4
12	136 PTS	2.52	7.3	4.6
12.5	141 PTS	2.42	7.6	4.8
13	147 PTS	2.33	7.9	5
13.5	153 PTS	2.24	8.2	5.2
14	159 PTS	2.16	8.5	5.4
15	14.2 PI	2.01	9.2	5.8
16	15.1 PI	1.89	9.8	6.1
17	16.1 PI	1.77	10.4	6.5
18	17 PI	1.67	11	6.9
19	18 PI	1.59	11.6	7.3
20	18.9 PI	1.51	12.2	7.7
21	19.9 PI	1.43	12.8	8
22	20.8 PI	1.37	13.4	8.4
23	21.8 PI	1.31	14	8.8
24	22.7 PI	1.25	14.6	9.2
25	23.7 PI	1.2	15.2	9.6
26	24.6 PI	1.16	15.9	10
27	25.6 PI	1.11	16.5	10.3
28	26.6 PI	1.07	17.1	10.7
29	27.5 PI	1.04	17.7	11.1
30	28.5 PI	1	18.3	11.5
31	29.4 PI	.97	18.9	11.9
32	30.4 PI	.94	19.5	12.3
33	31.3 PI	.91	20.1	12.7
34	32.3 PI	.88	20.7	13
35	33.2 PI	.86	21.3	13.4
36	34.2 PI	.83	22	13.8
37	35.1 PI	.81	22.6	14.2
38	36.1 PI	.79	23.2	14.6
39	37 PI	.77	23.8	15
40	38 PI	.75	24.4	15.3
41	38.9 PI	.73	25	15.7
42	39.9 PI	.71	25.6	16.1
43	40.8 PI	.7	26.2	16.5
44	41.8 PI	.68	26.8	16.9
45	42.8 PI	.67	27.5	17.3
46	43.7 PI	.65	28.1	17.6
47	44.7 PI	.64	28.7	18
48	45.6 PI	.62	29.3	18.4
49	46.6 PI	.61	29.9	18.8
50	47.5 PI	.6	30.5	19.2
51	48.5 PI	.59	31.1	19.6
52	49.4 PI	.58	31.7	19.9
53	50.4 PI	.57	32.3	20.3
54	51.3 PI	.56	32.9	20.7
55	52.3 PI	.55	33.6	21.1
56	53.2 PI	.54	34.2	21.5
57	54.2 PI	.53	34.8	21.8
58	55.1 PI	.52	35.4	22.2
59	56.1 PI	.51	36	22.6
60	57.1 PI	.5	36.6	23
61	58 PI	.49	37.2	23.4
62	59 PI	.48	37.8	23.8
63	59.9 PI	.48	38.4	24.2
64	60.9 PI	.47	39	24.5
65	61.8 PI	.46	39.6	24.9
66	62.8 PI	.45	40.3	25.3
67	63.7 PI	.45	40.9	25.7
68	64.7 PI	.44	41.5	26.1
69	65.6 PI	.43	42.1	26.5
70	66.6 PI	.43	42.7	26.8
71	67.5 PI	.42	43.3	27.2
72	68.5 PI	.42	43.9	27.6

HELVETICA (LINOTRON #202)

SIZE	AL/LENGTH	CHS/PI	CAP'X'	LC'X'
6	75 PTS	4.56	4.3	3.2
6.5	81 PTS	4.2	4.7	3.5
7	88 PTS	3.9	5	3.7
7.5	94 PTS	3.64	5.4	4
8	100 PTS	3.41	5.7	4.3
8.5	107 PTS	3.2	6.1	4.5
9	113 PTS	3.02	6.5	4.8
9.5	119 PTS	2.86	6.8	5.1
10	126 PTS	2.72	7.2	5.3
10.5	132 PTS	2.59	7.5	5.6
11	138 PTS	2.47	7.9	5.9
11.5	145 PTS	2.36	8.2	6.1
12	151 PTS	2.26	8.6	6.4
12.5	157 PTS	2.17	9	6.7
13	164 PTS	2.09	9.3	6.9
13.5	170 PTS	2.01	9.7	7.2
14	177 PTS	1.94	10	7.5
15	15.8 PI	1.81	10.8	8
16	16.8 PI	1.69	11.5	8.5
17	17.9 PI	1.59	12.2	9.1
18	18.9 PI	1.5	12.9	9.6
19	20 PI	1.43	13.6	10.1
20	21.1 PI	1.35	14.3	10.7
21	22.1 PI	1.29	15.1	11.2
22	23.2 PI	1.23	15.8	11.7
23	24.2 PI	1.18	16.5	12.3
24	25.3 PI	1.13	17.2	12.8
25	26.3 PI	1.08	17.9	13.3
26	27.4 PI	1.04	18.6	13.9
27	28.5 PI	1	19.4	14.4
28	29.5 PI	.97	20.1	14.9
29	30.6 PI	.93	20.8	15.5
30	31.6 PI	.9	21.5	16
31	32.7 PI	.87	22.2	16.5
32	33.7 PI	.84	22.9	17.1
33	34.8 PI	.82	23.7	17.6
34	35.9 PI	.79	24.4	18.1
35	36.9 PI	.77	25.1	18.7
36	38 PI	.75	25.8	19.2
37	39 PI	.73	26.5	19.7
38	40.1 PI	.71	27.2	20.3
39	41.1 PI	.69	28	20.8
40	42.2 PI	.68	28.7	21.3
41	43.3 PI	.66	29.4	21.9
42	44.3 PI	.64	30.1	22.4
43	45.4 PI	.63	30.8	22.9
44	46.4 PI	.61	31.5	23.5
45	47.5 PI	.6	32.3	24
46	48.5 PI	.59	33	24.5
47	49.6 PI	.57	33.7	25.1
48	50.7 PI	.56	34.4	25.6
49	51.7 PI	.55	35.1	26.1
50	52.8 PI	.54	35.8	26.7
51	53.8 PI	.53	36.6	27.2
52	54.9 PI	.52	37.3	27.7
53	55.9 PI	.51	38	28.3
54	57 PI	.5	38.7	28.8
55	58.1 PI	.49	39.4	29.3
56	59.1 PI	.48	40.1	29.9
57	60.2 PI	.47	40.9	30.4
58	61.2 PI	.47	41.6	30.9
59	62.3 PI	.46	42.3	31.5
60	63.3 PI	.45	43	32
61	64.4 PI	.44	43.7	32.5
62	65.5 PI	.44	44.4	33.1
63	66.5 PI	.43	45.2	33.6
64	67.6 PI	.42	45.9	34.1
65	68.6 PI	.42	46.6	34.7
66	69.7 PI	.41	47.3	35.2
67	70.7 PI	.4	48	35.7
68	71.8 PI	.4	48.7	36.3
69	72.9 PI	.39	49.5	36.8
70	73.9 PI	.39	50.2	37.3
71	75 PI	.38	50.9	37.9
72	76 PI	.37	51.6	38.4

PALATINO (LINOTRON #202)

SIZE	AL/LENGTH	CHS/PI	CAP'X'	LC'X'
6	80 PTS	4.28	4.2	2.8
6.5	87 PTS	3.94	4.6	3.1
7	93 PTS	3.66	4.9	3.3
7.5	100 PTS	3.41	5.3	3.6
8	107 PTS	3.2	5.7	3.8
8.5	114 PTS	3.01	6	4
9	120 PTS	2.84	6.4	4.3
9.5	127 PTS	2.69	6.7	4.5
10	134 PTS	2.56	7.1	4.7
10.5	140 PTS	2.43	7.4	5
11	147 PTS	2.32	7.8	5.2
11.5	154 PTS	2.22	8.1	5.4
12	161 PTS	2.13	8.5	5.7
12.5	167 PTS	2.04	8.8	5.9
13	174 PTS	1.96	9.2	6.2
13.5	181 PTS	1.89	9.5	6.4
14	188 PTS	1.82	9.9	6.6
15	16.7 PI	1.7	10.6	7.1
16	17.9 PI	1.6	11.3	7.6
17	19 PI	1.5	12	8
18	20.1 PI	1.42	12.7	8.5
19	21.2 PI	1.34	13.4	9
20	22.3 PI	1.28	14.1	9.5
21	23.5 PI	1.21	14.8	9.9
22	24.6 PI	1.16	15.5	10.4
23	25.7 PI	1.11	16.3	10.9
24	26.8 PI	1.06	17	11.4
25	27.9 PI	1.02	17.7	11.8
26	29.1 PI	.98	18.4	12.3
27	30.2 PI	.94	19.1	12.8
28	31.3 PI	.91	19.8	13.3
29	32.4 PI	.88	20.5	13.7
30	33.5 PI	.85	21.2	14.2
31	34.7 PI	.82	21.9	14.7
32	35.8 PI	.8	22.6	15.1
33	36.9 PI	.77	23.3	15.6
34	38 PI	.75	24	16.1
35	39.1 PI	.73	24.7	16.6
36	40.3 PI	.71	25.4	17
37	41.4 PI	.69	26.1	17.5
38	42.5 PI	.67	26.9	18
39	43.6 PI	.65	27.6	18.5
40	44.7 PI	.64	28.3	18.9
41	45.9 PI	.62	29	19.4
42	47 PI	.61	29.7	19.9
43	48.1 PI	.59	30.4	20.4
44	49.2 PI	.58	31.1	20.8
45	50.3 PI	.57	31.8	21.3
46	51.5 PI	.55	32.5	21.8
47	52.6 PI	.54	33.2	22.2
48	53.7 PI	.53	33.9	22.7
49	54.8 PI	.52	34.6	23.2
50	55.9 PI	.51	35.3	23.7
51	57.1 PI	.5	36	24.1
52	58.2 PI	.49	36.7	24.6
53	59.3 PI	.48	37.5	25.1
54	60.4 PI	.47	38.2	25.6
55	61.5 PI	.46	38.9	26
56	62.7 PI	.45	39.6	26.5
57	63.8 PI	.45	40.3	27
58	64.9 PI	.44	41	27.5
59	66 PI	.43	41.7	27.9
60	67.1 PI	.42	42.4	28.4
61	68.3 PI	.42	43.1	28.9
62	69.4 PI	.41	43.8	29.3
63	70.5 PI	.4	44.5	29.8
64	71.6 PI	.4	45.2	30.3
65	72.7 PI	.39	45.9	30.8
66	73.9 PI	.39	46.6	31.2
67	75 PI	.38	47.3	31.7
68	76.1 PI	.37	48.1	32.2
69	77.2 PI	.37	48.8	32.7
70	78.3 PI	.36	49.5	33.1
71	79.5 PI	.36	50.2	33.6
72	80.6 PI	.35	50.9	34.1

SERIF GOTHIC LIGHT (LINOTRON #202)

SIZE	AL/LENGTH	CHS/PI	CAP'X'	LC'X'
6	73 PTS	4.72	4.2	2.9
6.5	79 PTS	4.34	4.5	3.1
7	85 PTS	4.02	4.9	3.4
7.5	91 PTS	3.75	5.3	3.6
8	98 PTS	3.51	5.6	3.9
8.5	104 PTS	3.3	6	4.1
9	110 PTS	3.11	6.3	4.4
9.5	116 PTS	2.94	6.7	4.6
10	123 PTS	2.79	7	4.8
10.5	129 PTS	2.66	7.4	5.1
11	135 PTS	2.53	7.7	5.3
11.5	141 PTS	2.42	8.1	5.6
12	148 PTS	2.32	8.4	5.8
12.5	154 PTS	2.22	8.8	6
13	160 PTS	2.14	9.1	6.3
13.5	166 PTS	2.06	9.5	6.5
14	173 PTS	1.98	9.8	6.8
15	15.4 PI	1.85	10.5	7.3
16	16.5 PI	1.73	11.2	7.7
17	17.5 PI	1.63	11.9	8.2
18	18.5 PI	1.54	12.6	8.7
19	19.6 PI	1.46	13.3	9.2
20	20.6 PI	1.38	14	9.7
21	21.7 PI	1.32	14.7	10.2
22	22.7 PI	1.26	15.4	10.6
23	23.8 PI	1.2	16.1	11.1
24	24.8 PI	1.15	16.8	11.6
25	25.8 PI	1.1	17.5	12.1
26	26.9 PI	1.06	18.2	12.6
27	27.9 PI	1.02	18.9	13.1
28	29 PI	.98	19.6	13.5
29	30 PI	.95	20.3	14
30	31 PI	.92	21	14.5
31	32.1 PI	.89	21.7	15
32	33.1 PI	.86	22.4	15.5
33	34.2 PI	.83	23.1	16
34	35.2 PI	.81	23.8	16.4
35	36.3 PI	.79	24.5	16.9
36	37.3 PI	.76	25.2	17.4
37	38.3 PI	.74	25.9	17.9
38	39.4 PI	.72	26.6	18.4
39	40.4 PI	.71	27.3	18.9
40	41.5 PI	.69	28	19.3
41	42.5 PI	.67	28.7	19.8
42	43.5 PI	.65	29.4	20.3
43	44.6 PI	.64	30.1	20.8
44	45.6 PI	.62	30.8	21.3
45	46.7 PI	.61	31.5	21.8
46	47.7 PI	.6	32.2	22.2
47	48.8 PI	.58	32.9	22.7
48	49.8 PI	.57	33.6	23.2
49	50.8 PI	.56	34.3	23.7
50	51.9 PI	.55	35	24.2
51	52.9 PI	.54	35.7	24.7
52	54 PI	.53	36.4	25.1
53	55 PI	.52	37.1	25.6
54	56 PI	.51	37.8	26.1
55	57.1 PI	.5	38.5	26.6
56	58.1 PI	.49	39.2	27.1
57	59.2 PI	.48	39.9	27.6
58	60.2 PI	.47	40.6	28
59	61.3 PI	.47	41.3	28.5
60	62.3 PI	.46	42	29
61	63.3 PI	.45	42.7	29.5
62	64.4 PI	.44	43.4	30
63	65.4 PI	.44	44.1	30.5
64	66.5 PI	.43	44.8	30.9
65	67.5 PI	.42	45.5	31.4
66	68.5 PI	.42	46.2	31.9
67	69.6 PI	.41	46.9	32.4
68	70.6 PI	.4	47.6	32.9
69	71.7 PI	.4	48.3	33.4
70	72.7 PI	.39	49	33.8
71	73.8 PI	.39	49.7	34.3
72	74.8 PI	.38	50.4	34.8

SOUVENIR LIGHT (LINOTRON #202)

SIZE	AL/LENGTH	CHS/PI	CAP'X'	LC'X'
6	73 PTS	4.68	4.4	2.8
6.5	79 PTS	4.32	4.8	3
7	85 PTS	4.01	5.1	3.3
7.5	91 PTS	3.74	5.5	3.5
8	98 PTS	3.5	5.9	3.7
8.5	104 PTS	3.3	6.2	4
9	110 PTS	3.11	6.6	4.2
9.5	116 PTS	2.95	7	4.4
10	122 PTS	2.8	7.3	4.7
10.5	128 PTS	2.66	7.7	4.9
11	135 PTS	2.54	8.1	5.1
11.5	141 PTS	2.43	8.4	5.4
.12	147 PTS	2.33	8.8	5.6
12.5	153 PTS	2.23	9.2	5.8
13	159 PTS	2.15	9.5	6.1
13.5	165 PTS	2.07	9.9	6.3
14	172 PTS	1.99	10.3	6.5
15	15.3 PI	1.86	11	7
16	16.3 PI	1.74	11.7	7.5
17	17.4 PI	1.64	12.5	7.9
18	18.4 PI	1.55	13.2	8.4
19	19.4 PI	1.47	13.9	8.9
20	20.4 PI	1.39	14.7	9.3
21	21.5 PI	1.33	15.4	9.8
22	22.5 PI	1.27	16.1	10.3
23	23.5 PI	1.21	16.9	10.7
24	24.6 PI	1.16	17.6	11.2
25	25.6 PI	1.11	18.3	11.7
26	26.6 PI	1.07	19.1	12.1
27	27.6 PI	1.03	19.8	12.6
28	28.7 PI	.99	20.5	13.1
29	29.7 PI	.96	21.3	13.5
30	30.7 PI	.93	22	14
31	31.7 PI	.9	22.7	14.5
32	32.8 PI	.87	23.5	14.9
33	33.8 PI	.84	24.2	15.4
34	34.8 PI	.82	24.9	15.9
35	35.8 PI	.8	25.7	16.3
36	36.9 PI	.77	26.4	16.8
37	37.9 PI	.75	27.1	17.3
38	38.9 PI	.73	27.9	17.7
39	39.9 PI	.72	28.6	18.2
40	41 PI	.7	29.3	18.7
41	42 PI	.68	30.1	19.1
42	43 PI	.66	30.8	19.6
43	44 PI	.65	31.5	20.1
44	45.1 PI	.63	32.3	20.5
45	46.1 PI	.62	33	21
46	47.1 PI	.6	33.7	21.5
47	48.2 PI	.59	34.5	21.9
48	49.2 PI	.58	35.2	22.4
49	50.2 PI	.57	35.9	22.9
50	51.2 PI	.56	36.7	23.3
51	52.3 PI	.55	37.4	23.8
52	53.3 PI	.53	38.1	24.3
53	54.3 PI	.52	38.9	24.7
54	55.3 PI	.52	39.6	25.2
55	56.4 PI	.51	40.3	25.7
56	57.4 PI	.5	41.1	26.1
57	58.4 PI	.49	41.8	26.6
58	59.4 PI	.48	42.5	27.1
59	60.5 PI	.47	43.3	27.5
60	61.5 PI	.46	44	28
61	62.5 PI	.46	44.7	28.5
62	63.5 PI	.45	45.5	28.9
63	64.6 PI	.44	46.2	29.4
64	65.6 PI	.43	46.9	29.9
65	66.6 PI	.43	47.7	30.3
66	67.6 PI	.42	48.4	30.8
67	68.7 PI	.42	49.1	31.3
68	69.7 PI	.41	49.9	31.7
69	70.7 PI	.4	50.6	32.2
70	71.8 PI	.4	51.3	32.7
71	72.8 PI	.39	52.1	33.1
72	73.8 PI	.39	52.8	33.6

TIMES ROMAN (LINOTRON #202)

SIZE	AL/LENGTH	CHS/PI	CAP'X'	LC'X'
6	78 PTS	4.38	4.2	2.8
6.5	84 PTS	4.05	4.5	3
7	91 PTS	3.77	4.9	3.3
7.5	97 PTS	3.52	5.3	3.5
8	103 PTS	3.31	5.6	3.7
8.5	110 PTS	3.12	6	4
9	116 PTS	2.95	6.3	4.2
9.5	122 PTS	2.79	6.7	4.4
10	129 PTS	2.66	7	4.7
10.5	135 PTS	2.53	7.4	4.9
11	141 PTS	2.42	7.7	5.1
11.5	148 PTS	2.31	8.1	5.4
12	154 PTS	2.22	8.4	5.6
12.5	160 PTS	2.13	8.8	5.8
13	167 PTS	2.05	9.1	6.1
13.5	173 PTS	1.98	9.5	6.3
14	180 PTS	1.91	9.8	6.5
15	16 PI	1.78	10.5	7
16	17.1 PI	1.67	11.2	7.5
17	18.1 PI	1.57	11.9	7.9
18	19.2 PI	1.49	12.6	8.4
19	20.2 PI	1.41	13.3	8.9
20	21.3 PI	1.34	14	9.3
21	22.4 PI	1.27	14.7	9.8
22	23.4 PI	1.22	15.4	10.3
23	24.5 PI	1.16	16.1	10.7
24	25.5 PI	1.12	16.8	11.2
25	26.6 PI	1.07	17.5	11.7
26	27.6 PI	1.03	18.2	12.1
27	28.7 PI	.99	18.9	12.6
28	29.8 PI	.96	19.6	13.1
29	30.8 PI	.92	20.3	13.5
30	31.9 PI	.89	21	14
31	32.9 PI	.87	21.7	14.5
32	34 PI	.84	22.4	14.9
33	35 PI	.81	23.1	15.4
34	36.1 PI	.79	23.8	15.9
35	37.2 PI	.77	24.5	16.3
36	38.2 PI	.75	25.2	16.8
37	39.3 PI	.73	25.9	17.3
38	40.3 PI	.71	26.6	17.7
39	41.4 PI	.69	27.3	18.2
40	42.4 PI	.67	28	18.7
41	43.5 PI	.66	28.7	19.1
42	44.6 PI	.64	29.4	19.6
43	45.6 PI	.62	30.1	20.1
44	46.7 PI	.61	30.8	20.5
45	47.7 PI	.6	31.5	21
46	48.8 PI	.58	32.2	21.5
47	49.8 PI	.57	32.9	21.9
48	50.9 PI	.56	33.6	22.4
49	52 PI	.55	34.3	22.9
50	53 PI	.54	35	23.3
51	54.1 PI	.53	35.7	23.8
52	55.1 PI	.52	36.4	24.3
53	56.2 PI	.51	37.1	24.7
54	57.3 PI	.5	37.8	25.2
55	58.3 PI	.49	38.5	25.7
56	59.4 PI	.48	39.2	26.1
57	60.4 PI	.47	39.9	26.6
58	61.5 PI	.46	40.6	27.1
59	62.5 PI	.46	41.3	27.5
60	63.6 PI	.45	42	28
61	64.7 PI	.44	42.7	28.5
62	65.7 PI	.43	43.4	28.9
63	66.8 PI	.43	44.1	29.4
64	67.8 PI	.42	44.8	29.9
65	68.9 PI	.41	45.5	30.3
66	69.9 PI	.41	46.2	30.8
67	71 PI	.4	46.9	31.3
68	72.1 PI	.4	47.6	31.7
69	73.1 PI	.39	48.3	32.2
70	74.2 PI	.38	49	32.7
71	75.2 PI	.38	49.7	33.1
72	76.3 PI	.37	50.4	33.6

POINTS TO MILLIMETERS

Points	Millimeters
.5	.1753
1.	.3505
1.5	.5258
2.	.7010
2.5	.8763
3.	1.0515
3.5	1.2268
4.	1.4020
4.5	1.5773
5.	1.7525
5.5	1.9278
6.	2.1030
6.5	2.2783
7.	2.4535
7.5	2.6288
8.	2.8040
8.5	2.9793
9.	3.1545
9.5	3.3298
10.	3.5050
10.5	3.6803
11.	3.8555
11.5	4.0308
12.	4.2060

MILLIMETERS TO POINTS

Millimeters	Points
.1	.2853
.2	.5706
.3	.8559
.4	1.1412
.5	1.4265
.6	1.7118
.7	1.9971
.8	2.2825
.9	2.5678
1.0	2.8531
1.1	3.1384
1.2	3.4237
1.3	3.7090
1.4	3.9943
1.5	4.2796
1.6	4.5649
1.7	4.8502
1.8	5.1355
1.9	5.4208
2.0	5.7061
2.1	5.9914
2.2	6.2767
2.3	6.5621
2.4	6.8474
2.5	7.1327
2.6	7.4180
2.7	7.7033
2.8	7.9886
2.9	8.2739
3.0	8.5592
3.1	8.8445
3.2	9.1298
3.3	9.4151
3.4	9.7004
3.5	9.9857
3.6	10.2710
3.7	10.5563
3.8	10.8417
3.9	11.1270
4.0	11.4123
4.1	11.6976
4.2	11.9829
4.3	12.2682
4.4	12.5535

This book was set in Harris Fototronic CRT
Times Roman and Vega (Helvetica) under computer control
by Science Typographers, Medford, Long Island, New York.